Oracle Performance Troubleshooting

With Dictionary Internals SQL & Tuning Scripts

Robin Schumacher

Hope this helps!

RAMPANT
TECHPRESS

This book is dedicated to the most important people in my life.
To Jesus Christ for my eternal salvation, to my wonderful wife Laura who is more than I could ever ask for and certainly more than I deserve and to the two most precious little girls on the planet — Hannah and Claire — for being daddy's sweethearts and for causing a permanent smile to forever be affixed to my face.

Oracle Performance Troubleshooting
With Dictionary Internals SQL & Tuning Scripts

By Robin Schumacher

Copyright © 2003 by Rampant TechPress. All rights reserved.

Printed in the United States of America.

Published by Rampant TechPress, Kittrell, North Carolina, USA

Oracle In-Focus Series: Book #5

Editors: Bob Strickland, John Lavender, Linda Webb

Production Editor: Teri Wade

Cover Design: Bryan Hoff

Printing History:

> May 2003 for First Edition

Oracle, Oracle7, Oracle8, Oracle8i and Oracle9i are trademarks of Oracle Corporation. *Oracle In-Focus* is a registered Trademark of Rampant TechPress.

Many of the designations used by computer vendors to distinguish their products are claimed as Trademarks. All names known to Rampant TechPress to be trademark names appear in this text as initial caps.

The information provided by the authors of this work is believed to be accurate and reliable, but because of the possibility of human error by our authors and staff, Rampant TechPress cannot guarantee the accuracy or completeness of any information included in this work and is not responsible for any errors, omissions or inaccurate results obtained from the use of information or scripts in this work.

ISBN: 0-9727513-4-3

Library of Congress Control Number: 2003105334

Table of Contents

Using the Online Code Depot 1
Conventions Used in this Book 2
Acknowledgements 4
Preface 6

CHAPTER 1 8

Accurately Measuring Performance 8
Modeling Peak Efficiency 9
Modeling Availability 10
Modeling Speed 13
Model Dependencies 18
Conclusion 26

CHAPTER 2 27

Applying Performance Methodologies 27
Ratio-Based Analysis 29
Bottleneck Analysis 34
Combining Bottleneck and Ratio Analysis 43
Workload Analysis 49
Conclusion 50

CHAPTER 3 52

Correcting Foundational Flaws 52
Why is Physical Design Overlooked? 54
The Number One Performance Myth 56
The Link between Performance Monitoring and Physical Design 57
Making the Biggest Performance Impact 61
Spotting Physical Design Flaws 65
The Dream Software Tool for Design 69
Conclusion 73

CHAPTER 4 75

Optimizing Storage 75
The Contribution of Storage to Performance 76
Storage Design Considerations 78
   The Coming Physical I/O Crisis 80
Avoiding Database Downtime 88
Critical Storage Headaches to Avoid 102
   Fragmentation Types 103

    Detecting Tablespace Fragmentation 105
    Eliminating Tablespace Fragmentation 111
    Detecting Object Fragmentation 113
    Correcting Object Fragmentation 116
  Removing Storage-related Performance Vampires 116
    Table Diagnostics 117
    Index Diagnostics 122
    Database Maintenance Plans 127
  Conclusion 128

CHAPTER 5 .... **129**

  Maximizing Memory 129
  Getting a Handle on Memory Usage 131
    The Buffer Cache Hit Ratio – Still Worthwhile? 139
    Getting Advice on the Buffer Cache 143
    How to Keep Data Where You Want It 146
    Exploiting the New 9i Data Caches 147
    Other Interesting Buffer Cache Metrics 149
    Looking into the Shared Pool 151
    Getting More Details on Shared Pool Usage 153
    How to Keep Code Where You Want It 157
    More Shared Pool Metrics 159
    Examining the Log Buffer 161
  Investigating Session Memory Usage 162
  Miscellaneous Memory Issues 167
  Conclusion 171

CHAPTER 6 .... **173**

  Pinpointing I/O Hotspots 173
  Global Basic queries 174
  Determine Global Object Access Patterns 178
  Examine Storage-level Statistics 181
  Locating Hot I/O Objects 185
  Find the Current I/O Session Bandits 188
  Miscellaneous I/O Considerations 193
  Conclusion 198

CHAPTER 7 .... **199**

  Workload Analysis Part 1 - Uncovering Problem Sessions 199
  Uncovering Security Holes 200
  Finding Storage Hogs 203
  Locating Top Resource Sessions 207
  Pinpointing Sessions with Problem SQL 219

Conclusion..222

CHAPTER 8 .... **223**

Workload Analysis Part 2 - Identifying Problem SQL.............................223
What is 'Bad SQL'? 225
Pinpointing Bad SQL..226
New Techniques for Analyzing SQL Execution......................................232
SQL Tuning Roadmap 236
Look for Object-based Solutions *247*
Conclusion..250
Index..251

Using the Online Code Depot

Your purchase of this book provides you with complete access to the online code depot that contains the sample tests and answers.

All of the job questions in this book are located at the following URL:

rampant.cc/perf.htm

All of the sample tests in this book will be available for download to you in a zip format, ready to load and use on your database.

If you need technical assistance in downloading or accessing the scripts, please contact Rampant TechPress at info@rampant.cc.

Conventions Used in this Book

It is critical for any technical publication to follow rigorous standards and employ consistent punctuation conventions to make the text easy to read.

However, this is not an easy task. Within Oracle there are many types of notation that can confuse a reader. Some Oracle utilities such as STATSPACK and TKPROF are always spelled in CAPITAL letters, while Oracle parameters and procedures have varying naming conventions in the Oracle documentation. It is also important to remember that many Oracle commands are case sensitive, and are always left in their original executable for, and never altered with italics or capitalization.

Hence, all Rampant TechPress books following the following conventions:

Parameters - All Oracle parameters will be *lowercase italics*. Exception to this rule will be parameter arguments that are commonly capitalized (KEEP pool, TKPROF), and those will be left in ALL CAPS.

Variables – All PL/SQL program variables and arguments will also remain in lowercase italics (*dbms_job, dbms_utility*).

Tables & dictionary objects – All data dictionary objects are referenced in lowercase italics (*dba_indexes, v$sql*). This include all v$ and x$ views (*x$kcbcbh, v$parameter*) and dictionary views (*dba_tables, user_indexes*).

SQL – All SQL is formatted for easy use in the code depot, and all SQL is displayed in lowercase. The main SQL terms, (select, from, where, group by, order by, having) will always appear on a separate line.

Programs & Products – All products and programs that are known to the author are capitalized according the vendor specifications (IBM, DBXray, etc). All names known to Rampant TechPress to be trademark names appear in this text as initial caps. References to UNIX are always made in uppercase.

Acknowledgements

This type of highly technical reference book requires the dedicated efforts of many people. Even though we are the authors, our work ends when we deliver the content. After each chapter is delivered, several Oracle DBAs carefully review and correct the technical content. After the technical review, experienced copy editors polish the grammar and syntax. The finished work is then reviewed as page proofs and turned-over to the production manager who arranges the creation of the online code depot and managers the cover art, printing distribution and warehousing.

I need to thank and acknowledge everyone who helped bring this book to fruition:

John Lavender, for the production management, including the coordination of the cover art, page proofing, printing and distribution.

Bob Strickland, for his excellent copyediting and format checking services.

Teri Wade, for her expert help in the production of the page proofs.

Bryan Hoff, for his exceptional cover design and graphics.

Janet Burleson, for her assistance in the web site, the creation of the code depot, and the online shopping cart for this book.

Linda Webb, for her expert page proofing services.

With sincerest thanks,

Robin Schumacher

Preface

More than ever before, today's Oracle DBA faces a database farm that is growing both in physical size and actual numbers. To keep these databases up and performing at exceptional levels, the database administrator needs more than a cobbled together set of scripts that they use to (hopefully) verify that everything is in order.

Such an approach does not scale or offer the protection that critical business applications need. Instead, a DBA needs a solid methodology that can be implemented and replicated to one or thousands of databases to ensure peak availability and performance.

This book introduces both strategic and tactical methodologies that the DBA can take and utilize in a proactive manner to guarantee success in the fight for maximum availability and performance. It begins by introducing the proper ways to gauge and measure database performance, and then highlights how to put the right foundation in place for continuous database success.

It then takes the reader into the strategies that can be used to quickly take the guesswork out of knowing what databases really need attention in their organization. From there, it demonstrates how to avoid the major killers of database availability and performance by providing proven techniques that work in the real world.

Each chapter turns the spotlight on database performance and shows how to work with surgical precision to locate hidden headaches that threaten exceptional database performance.

It is my hope that this book will provide you with insight that helps your database run as faster than your most demanding user expects.

Chapter 1

Accurately Measuring Performance

Probably every database professional would like to be thought of as a performance-tuning expert. Slow systems are the bane of existence for any critical business, and DBAs and developers alike constantly strive to improve their diagnostic skills. And, why shouldn't they? The IT consultants who make the really big money are the ones who can take a lethargic system and quickly turn it into one that runs as fast as greased lightning.

But while there is certainly a lot of theory and knowledge flying back and forth in books, magazines, and database bulletin boards, the cold hard fact is the majority of database folks are confused over how they should really monitor a database to ensure peak efficiency.

To make matters worse, the continual march towards complexity of the major DBMS vendors, like Oracle, means that today's database professional must constantly stay abreast of new performance issues. Add to the mix that most DBAs must work cross-platform *and* that the number of databases they manage is skyrocketing, and you have the makings of a real mess.

Because of today's heavy reliance on database-driven systems, a database professional cannot waste time guessing at what might be causing a critical database to sputter and cough along like a Model T automobile. Instead, they need to understand the performance priorities of a database, and be able to quickly and proactively identify problems before they reach critical mass.

One of the best ways to understand such a thing is by *modeling* database performance. While you might be familiar with modeling a database design, the thought of creating a model of database performance might seem odd at first. Can something like this actually be done?

Modeling Peak Efficiency

Models represent the "big picture" of something on the surface and provide methods to drill down into the nitty-gritty of a subject. Data models, for example, are a way to succinctly communicate the aspects and aspect-relationships of a database in a way that even non-technical folks can (usually) understand.

A performance model is designed to do the same - communicate the total performance situation, using a direct method, in a way that both the experienced and novice database staff member can understand. A model of this nature should, for example, be able to quickly convey a total performance message so the DBA knows exactly where they stand and what their tuning priorities are. To accomplish this requires zeroing in on the major aspects that make up database performance and working downward from there.

Stating the obvious, it can be said that the goal of every database professional is to achieve peak efficiency in their database. And just what is "peak efficiency"? One way to define it is with the simple formula:

PEAK EFFICIENCY = AVAILABILITY + SPEED

The two large components of availability and speed combine to make or break any database system. This is true regardless of the underlying architecture of the database engine. DBAs need their databases to be up and their resources available to meet incoming requests; they also need the DBMS configured so that it can quickly handle all imposed system loads. It is much more complex under the covers than that, but it is also just as simple on the surface.

Your performance model, regardless of whether it is an Oracle database or other DBMS platform, begins with the two critical elements of availability and speed. These are the major components of any performance model. Find a way to quickly diagnose their success or failure, and you are on your way to working more efficiently.

Modeling Availability

Most professionals have the erroneous assumption that because a database is "up", it's available. Nothing could be further from the truth. There are many factors that you need to consider when modeling the availability portion of your performance model. Although other factors may play a part, the computation of database availability can be summed up in the equation:

TOTAL AVAILABILITY =
DATABASE ACCESSIBILITY +
RESOURCE AVAILABILITY

Each availability component is comprised of several sub-modules that must be measured. For database accessibility, there are two primary sub-modules.

Database Accessibility

There are two primary components that make up database accessibility:

- **Database "Readiness"** - This is what everyone thinks of when the question is asked, "Is the database up"? For Oracle, this equates to the instance being successfully started (background processes plus SGA structures), and to having all file structures accounted for and open.

- **Connectivity** – It's amazing how often people forget about the network side of the database. This does not mean LANs or TCP, but instead the required components that allow client connections into a database. For Oracle, this is the Listener process (working in conjunction with Oracle's networking software). If the listener is down or not functioning properly, your database might as well be down. The exception would be in situations where the clients work on the same machine as the server.

- The effect of a down listener is most often the same as a down database. Everything grinds to a halt.

Once database accessibility is established, the next area to peer into is resource availability.

Resource Availability

Like database accessibility, resource availability is made up of two factors.

Space Resource Availability

If a database does not have enough space to respond to data additions or modifications, then it is basically not available except for, perhaps, read operations. And, even these may be impacted if a disk sort is necessary to complete a select request. Fragmentation can also stop a database in its tracks if there are numerous free space extents inside a dictionary-managed tablespace that cannot be coalesced to meet a large free space request.

In addition to space concerns inside the database, space outside the database must also be taken into account, especially in this age where database files automatically grow to accommodate heavier-than-expected data loads. Make no mistake; space availability contributes a lot to the overall availability of any database. If you think this is untrue, then let your Oracle archive log destination run out of free space and see how smoothly things operate.

Object Resource Availability

In almost every database system, you will find a "hub" table that passes critical data in and out. Such systems are not hard to bring to a standstill. All it takes is a table being reorganized, an index becoming invalidated, or other such act, and true database availability goes out the window. Many other factors can affect resource availability as well.

If you have worked as a DBA a long time, you no doubt have occasionally encountered a blocking lock tree that is a mile long (one user blocking out everyone else), users waiting on memory structures to open up, or other contention events that affect overall efficiency. Total availability is heavily impacted by how available you keep the critical resources used by your database. It often affects the speed of your database as well (more on this in a moment).

Regardless of the database engine you are using, the performance model you need will consist of an availability sub-model that is comprised of the aforementioned elements. And for most critical businesses, availability is your first priority. Only after availability is confirmed, can you move on to speed.

The code depot key is	rudy

Modeling Speed

As already mentioned, all DBAs desire a fast and well-performing database. But, exactly how do you gauge database speed? Is a 99% *buffer cache hit ratio* the litmus test? Or, is it more complicated than that? Modeling the components of the speed sub-model is mostly straightforward, but there are some items that are difficult to measure that must be taken into account. To measure the success of the speed sub-model, the following equation will be used:

DATABASE SPEED = ACCESS EFFICIENCY + CODE EFFICIENCY + DESIGN SUCCESS

If the request completion rate and code efficiency ranking are at peak levels, and the database design is correct for the situation, then your database will be a top performer. As with the total availability model, the two main speed model components consist of several sub components.

Access Efficiency

There are two components that define access efficiency.

Data/Code Positioning

Data, code, and object definitions that reside in memory have a much higher return rate than objects that must first be retrieved from disk and placed into memory. The latest numbers on Oracle suggest that data can be accessed from RAM around 1,400 times faster than on physical disk.

While database engines differ in their layouts of the memory structures used to hold data and other necessary items, they all contain areas to speed the delivery of data and to lookup information. The percentage of times your database can serve information from memory, instead of disk, will contribute mightily toward your overall database speed.

Of course, hardware design counts here, with fast drives and load segmentation both playing a part. Contention at this level, however, normally falls under resource availability.

Access Path Effectiveness

The second determinant of access efficiency is the route the information must travel to be accessed. Index lookups vs. table scans must be taken into account to determine how well code has been written or how well the DBMS optimizer chooses the best path (design considerations also come into play here).

Small table scans should be overlooked, as it is often more efficient for a database to cache and scan a small table than to use any available indexing mechanisms. Another important factor that contributes to access path effectiveness is the consistent application of object demographics to the data dictionary.

Most DBAs have witnessed an access path, which worked well for objects with a certain volume of data, begin to fail when the demographics of those objects changed, and the database's optimizer was not informed of that fact. The final huge factor is I/O consumption - logical and physical. While physical I/O may take longer to accomplish a database request, a ton of logical I/O is not conducive to quick response time either.

Mitigating both should be a goal of the performance model. Even if your database is servicing requests well in memory, it might not matter if the code is not accessing the data properly or utilizing the right techniques to get only the data that is necessary.

This is where people who rely only on singular measures, like the buffer cache hit ratio, fail to properly measure performance. Yes, a user thread may sport a 98% cache hit ratio, but if that same thread used 500,000 buffer gets to produce a result that SQL could have achieved in 5,000 buffer gets, wouldn't overall speed be decreased?

Code efficiency is not simple to measure because individual SQL statements can be hard to track and trace, but there are a few components that will indicate positive or negative trends in this territory.

Code Efficiency

There are three areas to review with respect to code efficiency.

System Balance

Many rules of thumb turn out to be untrue, but the one saying that 80% of the problems in a database are caused by 10-20% of the users is right on the money. Rarely will you encounter a database where the majority of users and their SQL statements produce extreme code-related performance statistics. Instead, a few sessions and their accompanying SQL will be the ones degrading performance. That being the case, you can evaluate the percentage of code-related statistics (memory and disk I/O) of the current resource hogs vs. the system total and see how balanced the code is with respect to performance.

Code Reuse

Except in the most ad-hoc databases, code reuse should be encouraged and enforced. Depending on the DBMS engine, this can be accomplished in a variety of ways. With Oracle (as with most other platforms), procedural code can be maintained through the use of stored procedures and triggers.

Embedded SQL code in applications can also be used to ensure all user sessions are running the same code line.

Why is code reuse important? Obviously, myriads of untested and untuned SQL statements sent against a database have the potential to cause performance bottlenecks. In addition, the DBMS engine must work extra hard at parsing and security checks. Techniques outlined later in this book will help you accomplish code reuse without working up too much of a sweat.

Code Soundness/Validation

While it is difficult to gauge in a computational method how valid a piece of database code is, there are telltale signs an expert eye can look for. Long execution times of seemingly simple code can raise eyebrows, as can skyrocketing logical or physical I/O for code runs. In addition, the invalidation of code objects can cause terrible malfunctions in a system. There is simply no place for invalid code objects in a production system. Period.

Design Success

Most believe that code inefficiency is the number one cause of system problems. As has already been mentioned, a lot of rules of thumb turn out to be untrue, and this is one of them. The number one cause of performance-related problems, as well as system outages, is bad design. Tragically, this is not only the number one cause of speed and availability headaches, but is also the hardest to model in terms of declaring things good or bad overall.

For example, how can you easily tell if denormalizing a set of tables into one object will accelerate performance? In the world of RAID and fast I/O devices, how can you tell whether separating tables and indexes onto different physical drives will enhance speed, or if a bitmap index is needed on a large dimension-styled table?

Sadly, design success cannot be measured as easily or evaluated as quickly as the other components in the performance model. However, an upcoming chapter in this book will help you to identify physical design weaknesses that ultimately lead to reduced system performance.

Model Dependencies

The goal of this performance model (and any other model) is to communicate the total picture in an easily assimilated form. Therefore, the goal of the performance model is to provide the database professional with a global view of peak efficiency, either for a single database or a large number of installations. How will this be accomplished? Below is a bird's eye view of how you can globally gauge the peak efficiency of any database.

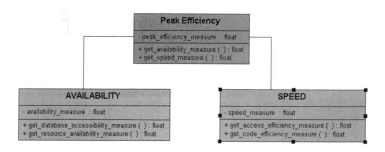

Figure 1.1 - Abbreviated global performance model representing the components of peak efficiency.

Before continuing, a comment needs to be made about Figure 1.1. To indicate peak efficiency, the model in Figure

1.1 uses a single peak efficiency measure to communicate the overall health of the database system. While this is certainly functional, you can also use the two measures derived from the availability and speed classes.

Why would you do this? The reason is that speed becomes irrelevant if total availability is not close to maximum levels. So, while using a single indicator to convey peak efficiency is more efficient if you are called upon to evaluate many systems at once, using the two measures independent of one another is possible as well (speed, of course, will not be a factor at all if the database is not accessible).

Following this vein, you should note that dependencies or relationships will exist in the performance model. As with any model, you rarely have objects that operate in an independent manner. The data modeling discipline, for example, frowns on entities left "dangling" in a model.

If they have no relationship with other entities in the data model being constructed, what business do they have in the model to begin with? Our performance model has relationships or dependencies that are of critical importance. Performance modeling succeeds where traditional performance monitoring fails because it takes into account the dependencies between the many performance classes and measures. Only when a DBA observes both (the measurements plus the effect each has on the other), will the true performance picture emerge.

It is a fact that you cannot measure peak efficiency simply by weighing availability and speed independent of one another. We have already stated that speed, as we have defined it, is of no concern in a down database. Yet if a database is accessible and resources are open to incoming requests, speed quickly becomes the primary focus of attention. Figure 1.2 displays the dependency links in the performance model.

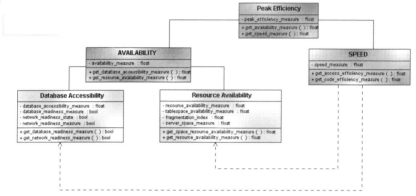

Figure 1.2 - Availability sub-model showing dependency links of speed to availability

Speed depends on the overall success of availability. However, the various dependencies will differ in their strength ratings, which is why the dependency links are drawn from the speed class to the availability sub-classes.

For example, if either the database or network is not in a ready state, no real work in a database can be performed. Speed's contribution to overall peak efficiency is totally negated. If, on the other hand, the database is accessible, but certain resources are unavailable (or nearly unavailable), speed may be impacted, but its contribution is not totally removed from the peak efficiency equation.

Of course, things like a stuck Oracle Archiver process or broken objects can produce nearly the same effect as a down database. But, common resource issues such as a tablespace nearing the end of its free space amount will not impact the speed class in our model nearly as much as database accessibility.

Still, resource availability has the ability to become quite a nasty showstopper in any database. It is a good bet that if your database is configured well and has the right design in place, but still has bottlenecks and slowdowns in the system, then the probable root cause will be waits and other resource blocks. Given poor resource availability, speed can again become a non-issue.

The Impact of Availability

How exactly does availability impact the performance model? The best way to comprehend this is to examine several different availability related situations and understand their impact.

Of course, the first thing to consider is what happens when the database or Oracle listener suddenly goes down. The peak efficiency of the database would be at zero (for a down database) or near zero (for a down listener that serves a client-server community).

Let's take another more involved example. While database accessibility components have the potential to cause a sudden, catastrophic drop in our peak efficiency model, other components can crash a system just as easily, but the end of the story will not be quite as abrupt. Take the case of one of the building blocks of resource availability - lock contention.

What happens to the model when lock contention rears its ugly head? That depends on a couple factors:

- The ratio of blocked users (database work) to overall connected sessions
- The duration of the bottleneck

Let's take the case of a database with 300 connected sessions and a current peak efficiency level of ninety-eight percent. Resource availability comes under fire when a single session grabs a resource and retains it for a short duration. Ten or so other sessions queue up quickly behind the blocking session and wait on the resource. The resource is released by the original blocking session in short order, which allows the other ten user threads to complete their work, and things return to normal. This brief encounter with lock contention would cause barely a hiccup in overall peak efficiency.

But, let's examine a lock contention case that is a little more severe. We will take another database that is running at ninety-eight percent peak efficiency but only has twenty user sessions performing work. One of the sessions locks a "hub" table, but before releasing the resource, the person is suddenly called into a long running meeting.

One by one, the remaining active sessions begin to queue up behind the blocking session until all are waiting. With both the blocked user to total connection ratio and lock duration measures working against the database, peak efficiency begins an overall downhill slide until it reaches zero or near-zero.

Where does speed fit into this picture? Again, you can see that it is negated totally by its dependency on our two main components that make up availability. Does it matter how high memory access measures are or that the access paths the optimizer is using to retrieve data couldn't be better?

Not in this case. Peak efficiency is in effect brought to a standstill by a single, escalating case of lock contention. The same thing could also be said of a transactional-heavy database suffering from a stuck Oracle Archiver process.

The point of this exercise is threefold. First, it serves to show that intelligent factors must be put into the performance model so each component and measure can accurately reflect the impact of circumstances that influence overall peak efficiency. In other words, the relationships/dependencies between measures play a huge role in communication performance.

Second, it underscores the critical nature of availability, and why it should always be the database administrator's number one priority.

But lastly and most importantly, it demonstrates the extremely important benefit of a performance model, which is to *represent performance as the end user is experiencing it*.

When a legitimate problem call comes in, many times the DBA will pull up a script or monitor and look at individual statistics that by themselves mean little or nothing. "Everything looks OK to me", the DBA says. But when pressed, they dig a little further, and they finally discover the bottleneck. How great it would be to instantly see the situation as your end user sees it.

The Impact of Speed

You may read this and think, "Well, speed doesn't seem to matter much at all in this model." Nothing could be further from the truth. If we have a database whose accessibility is nearly always ensured and whose resource availability is at peak levels around the clock, then does that mean peak efficiency is not at risk? No, of course not. Speed becomes the all-important component of the performance model *when and only when availability is under control*. After availability is assured, speed becomes king.

The phone call every administrator hates is the one that starts off with the complaint "Gee, the database sure seems to be running *slow*!" Of course, the network, application, and various other stress points couldn't be the problem - it always has to be the database. However, for the moment, remove all these other mitigating factors and say there actually is something going on at the database level.

What does *slow* mean? You are not getting the results from a SELECT statement back in reasonable time, the heavy-duty procedure that is doing some serious number crunching is not completing within its historical timeframes, or a process just seems to "hang"? The first two generally fall into the speed camp, while the last problem is typically one of resource availability.

Speed's impact on the overall peak efficiency model will seldom bring the overall measure to zero or near zero, but low speed ratings in your performance model can certainly make life miserable for those using such a database. How will you measure the overall impact of speed? First, understand that availability has no such dependencies tied to speed.

It is important to understand that speed, as it is defined in the performance model, does not come into play with things like how fast an incident of lock contention is resolved or the quickness at which a tablespace's free space is restored. In our model, speed is comprised of how quickly and effectively data is accessed, the efficiency of a database's code line, and the success of the physical database design.

As with availability, you cannot simply weight the various components and building blocks of speed in a static nature and be done. Some will count more than others, depending on the particular personality of the database and the total work being done at the moment. For example, nearly every database professional has watched a database have the air let out of its tires by a hog user who has fired off a massive procedure or runaway query.

Such a situation could signal problems in either the access or code efficiency components of the performance model. More than likely, it is code imbalance in the system, which would fall under the code efficiency portion of the model. While the problem procedure or query would temporarily depress measures like a buffer cache hit ratio or other memory statistics, the root cause of overall speed degradation is a piece of code out of balance with the normal work being conducted on a system.

Conclusion

Having a thorough understanding of the impact that each type of performance dependency has on your database is a great place to start when figuring out how to gauge database performance excellence. But, as it is so often the case, the devil is in the details when it comes to troubleshooting a complex database.

The rest of this book is devoted to helping you focus on, and drill down into, the major areas of database availability and speed so you can restore a troubled system to peak efficiency as quickly as possible. Whether it is uncovering physical design issues that are cramping overall performance, or pinpointing the table scans that are wreaking havoc at the I/O level, you will be given proven scripts and techniques that can be used to ferret out the root cause of performance slowdowns on any Oracle database.

To help you get a handle on how to diagnose an ailing database, the next chapter will introduce you to the two most prevalent styles of performance analysis: ratio-based and bottleneck. You will see how both analytic techniques provide ways to analyze the two components of your database performance model (availability and speed), and why each method is needed to help ensure your database is always up and running at peak efficiency.

Chapter 2

Applying Performance Methodologies

Database performance analysis can be carried out in many ways, and it seems that every database professional has their own preferred method. It can somewhat be likened to investment/stock analysis. There are many techniques that investors use to choose stocks for their portfolios, but most can be boiled down to two basic methods: fundamental and technical analysis.

Those who follow fundamental analysis look for things like continuous increases in a company's earnings per share, sales and revenue growth rates, profit margins, and other key factors that typically indicate a company's stock may be ready to rise. Proponents of technical analysis sneer at fundamentalists and insist that the way to pick winning stocks is by examining chart patterns of a company's stock, along with other market-leading indicators that can signal when to buy or sell.

Even though both techniques have their advocates, there are some investment professionals (most of them pretty good), who, instead of limiting themselves to one method, embrace *both*. The bursting of the tech bubble in the early 2000's taught technical enthusiasts one thing: a company's fundamentals and bottom line do matter.

And, fundamentalists learned that even a stock with outstanding corporate sales and revenue acceleration could be dragged down when its peers in the same industry group head south.

Like stock analysts, database performance analysts typically use one of two methods for examining the performance levels of a database.

- **Ratio-based Analysis** - This involves examining a number of key database ratios that can be used to indicate how well a database is running.

- **Bottleneck Analysis** - This seems to be more in vogue today, with many experts on database performance deriding those who still dare to practice any ratio-based analysis. Instead of using ratios, this methodology focuses on finding the things that cause the database to wait, and removing them where possible.

But, could it be that *both* analytical methods are needed to accurately diagnose a database's performance level? Just like smart investors who use both fundamental and technical analysis to make money in the stock market, should the smart database administrator use both ratio-based and bottleneck analysis to determine if a database is performing well?

That is the question this chapter strives to answer. Both techniques are examined and contrasted in detail. The best ways to practice both will be discussed, so you can combine both techniques to come up with one comprehensive and winning game plan that will serve you well in troubleshooting performance problems in Oracle databases. In addition to these methodologies, a third technique for analyzing database performance will also be presented.

The first technique to be examined is ratio-based analysis. Even if you have read current articles or white papers that say you should toss away this analytical method, you owe it to yourself to read the next section carefully and then see if you think that this currently maligned technique is really as bad as some people say.

Ratio-Based Analysis

Ratio-based analysis has been around for many years, and used to be the only technique database administrators utilized when they were called upon to diagnose the cause of a database slowdown. Using one or more cherished SQL scripts; the DBA would conduct an examination of key ratios such as database memory use, contention, I/O, network utilization, and others, to hopefully pinpoint the areas responsible for unacceptable performance.

Once a particular area was identified as suspect, the standard remedy was to increase the resources for that area (like memory), which oftentimes did the trick but occasionally failed to produce any real performance gain. Should ratio-based analysis still be used to assist in determining the overall health of a database, and if so, how should it be done?

When done right, ratio-based analysis definitely has a place in the DBA's performance-tuning arsenal. Performance ratios are very good roll-up mechanisms for busy DBAs, making analysis possible at a glance. Many DBAs have large database farms to contend with and cannot spend time checking detailed wait-based analysis outputs for each and every database they oversee.

Succinct performance ratios can assist in such situations by giving DBAs a few solid indicators that can be scanned quickly to see if any database needs immediate attention. Several chapters in this book will present a number of scripts that calculate many valuable ratios that you can use to get a handle on the performance of your database.

Deficiencies of Only Using a Wait-based Approach

Ratio-based analysis is also still viable because a pure wait-based approach will miss a number of critical items that indicate poor performance. For example, the wait events in Oracle do not do a very good job of identifying excessive disk sort activity, but the memory/disk sort ratio does.

Accurate Ratio Analysis Techniques

So, how does one accurately perform ratio-based analysis? While there are certainly many opinions as to what rules to follow, some standards should always be adhered. To begin with, many of the formulas that make up ratio-based analysis must be derived from delta measurements instead of cumulative statistics.

Many of the global ratios that a DBA will examine come from the *v$sysstat* performance view. This view maintains a count of all the occurrences (in the VALUE column) of a particular database incident (in the NAME column) since the database was brought up. For databases that are kept up for long periods of time, these values can grow quite large and will impact how a particular ratio is interpreted.

For example, let's take a look at one of the common queries used to report the database's buffer cache hit ratio:

```
select
   100 -
   100 *
   (round((sum (decode (name, 'physical reads', value, 0)) -
    sum (decode (name, 'physical reads direct', value, 0)))) /
   (sum (decode (name, 'db block gets', value, 1)) +
    sum (decode (name, 'consistent gets', value, 0)))),3))
 from
   sys.v_$sysstat
 where
   name in ('db block gets',  'consistent gets',
            'physical reads', 'physical reads direct');
```

If a database has been up for many weeks, the numbers representing the I/O statistics above will likely be enormous. The counts of block gets and consistent gets will be very large and in most systems, exceed the count of physical reads by a wide margin. Such a situation can skew the buffer cache hit ratio, if it is computed solely with cumulative value counts in *v$sysstat.*

If an inefficient query is issued that causes many physical reads, adding them to the *v$sysstat* counters will probably not cause a meaningful dip in the overall buffer cache hit ratio, so long as cumulative statistics are used. However, if delta statistics are used (taking, for a specified sampling period, the before and after counts of each statistic that make up the ratio), then the portrayal of the buffer cache hit ratio will be more current and accurate.

There are some ratios that do not rely on *v$sysstat,* and therefore, can be derived from current/cumulative values. One example of this is the blocking lock ratio, which computes the percentage of user sessions that are currently blocked on a system. Because locks in a database are repeatedly obtained and released, the ratio can be computed with cumulative numbers from several performance views, without the need for taking a before-and-after statistical snapshot.

In addition to using delta statistics to compute many of the key metrics in ratio-based performance analysis, DBAs must also be committed to examining all the database categories that contribute to its overall health and well-being. This can mean employing ratios and analytic percentages that have historically been neglected by DBAs.

For instance, many DBAs do not use ratios when examining their object structures in a database because they have not seen how such a technique can be applied to objects. However, ratio-based analysis can definitely be utilized to determine if objects like tables and indexes are disorganized. For example, finding the global percentage of tables that contain chained rows may help a DBA realize that he is not properly defining the table storage parameters in a dynamic database.

A final thing to remember about using ratio-based analysis is that while there are several rules of thumb that can be used as starting points in the evaluation of database performance, each database has an individual personality. Some hard and fast rules simply will not apply to every database.

For example, there was an e-commerce application that never saw its buffer cache hit ratio rise above 75%, a measure that would normally cause concern to most database analysts.

But oddly enough, none of the routinely vocal users of the system ever complained, response times always appeared good, the SQL seemed well-tuned, and adding more database buffers never seemed to improve the situation. So for that database, 75% was the benchmark to use for gauging the efficiency of logical/physical I/O activity in the database.

The Dangers of Blanket Ratios

The danger in using blanket ratio standards is that they can lead the DBA to take action haphazardly, often contributing nothing to the situation and sometimes even degrading performance. For example, one rule of thumb says that the library cache hit ratio should never fall below 95%, and if it does, the standard remedy is to increase the amount of memory assigned to the shared pool.

But this kind of lazy approach to performance tuning can actually lead to more problems. Oftentimes, a database that is very ad-hoc in nature will experience many queries that are almost always unique with respect to their WHERE predicates and the literals used as qualifying filters.

Such a thing naturally depresses the library cache hit ratio because the distinct queries cannot be reused by Oracle in the shared pool. If a DBA continuously increases the resources devoted to this type of shared pool, then performance can actually become worse, as Oracle must search an ever-increasing shared pool to check for a query match (that will not be found), with the end result being increased parse times. In such cases, a standard sized shared pool, with less than an ideal library cache hit ratio, is actually the best scenario (side note: the *cursor_sharing* parameter introduced in Oracle 8.1.6 can assist such a situation).

So, does ratio-based analysis still sound like old hat or do you think it can add value to a DBA's performance analysis arsenal? With an appreciation of ratio-based analysis, we are ready to continue into the next section and discover the ins-and-outs of bottleneck analysis.

Bottleneck Analysis

When an Oracle database is up and running, every connected process is either busy doing work or waiting to perform work. A process that is waiting may mean nothing in the overall scheme of things, or it can be an indicator that a database bottleneck exists.

This is where wait-based or bottleneck analysis comes into play. DBAs use this form of performance analysis to determine if perceived bottlenecks in a database are contributing to a performance problem.

Bottleneck analysis is a valid method of measuring performance because it helps a DBA track where a database has been spending its time. If latch contention or heavy table-scan activity has been dragging a database's performance down, a DBA can use bottleneck analysis to confirm the actual root cause.

Once one or more wait events or other bottlenecks have been pinpointed as possible performance vampires, the DBA can drill down and oftentimes discover a fair amount of detail about the sessions and objects that are causing the problem.

Prerequisites for Bottleneck Analysis

How does one correctly practice bottleneck or wait-based analysis? First, it is imperative that the *timed_statistics* initialization parameter be set to TRUE, if the Oracle wait events are to be examined. By default, this parameter is set to FALSE, which disallows the collection of wait times for each wait event defined in the Oracle engine.

For one to really understand the impact of wait events on database performance, the DBA needs to not only discover what the database is or has been waiting on but the durations of the waits. Having both allows a complete picture to be formed regarding the magnitude of wait-initiated performance degradations.

Almost all Oracle experts now agree that collecting time statistics adds little, if anything, to database overhead, so setting *timed_statistics* to TRUE should not be a worry. The parameter can be dynamically altered at both the system and session levels, so the database does not have to be shutdown and then restarted for the change to take effect. A simple *alter system set timed_statistics= true* should do the trick.

The next prerequisite to using bottleneck analysis is that certain wait events should be filtered out of any metrics used to diagnose performance bottlenecks. For example, Oracle will record a wait statistic that represents how long a particular user sits at their SQL*Plus prompt between each issued database request.

Such a statistic provides no real value to a DBA who is trying to figure out where a database bottleneck exists. Any SQL scripts that are used to collect database wait statistics should exclude such events. A listing of these Oracle events (normally dubbed "idle" events) to eliminate includes:

- lock element cleanup
- pmon timer
- rdbms ipc message
- smon timer
- SQL*Net message from client
- SQL*Net break/reset to client
- SQL*Net message to client
- SQL*Net more data to client
- dispatcher timer
- Null event
- parallel query dequeue wait
- parallel query idle wait - Slaves
- pipe get
- PL/SQL lock timer
- slave wait
- virtual circuit status

When collecting wait statistics, there are several levels of detail that a DBA can penetrate. The first level is the system view, which provides a global, cumulative snapshot of all the waits that have occurred on a system.

Viewing these numbers can help a DBA determine which wait events have caused the most commotion in a database thus far. A query that can be used to collect these metrics is the *syswaits.sql* script:

syswaits.sql

```
select
      event,
      total_waits,
      round(100 * (total_waits / sum_waits),2) pct_tot_waits,
      time_wait_sec,
      round(100 * (time_wait_sec / sum_secs),2) pct_secs_waits,
      total_timeouts,
      avg_wait_sec
from
(select
      event,
      total_waits,
      round((time_waited / 100),2) time_wait_sec,
      total_timeouts,
      round((average_wait / 100),2) avg_wait_sec
from
      sys.v_$system_event
where
      event not in
      ('lock element cleanup',
       'pmon timer',
       'rdbms ipc message',
       'smon timer',
       'SQL*Net message from client',
       'SQL*Net break/reset to client',
       'SQL*Net message to client',
       'SQL*Net more data to client',
       'dispatcher timer',
       'Null event',
       'parallel query dequeue wait',
       'parallel query idle wait - Slaves',
       'pipe get',
       'PL/SQL lock timer',
       'slave wait',
       'virtual circuit status',
       'WMON goes to sleep') and
      event not like 'DFS%' and
      event not like 'KXFX%'),
(select
```

```
        sum(total_waits) sum_waits,
        sum(round((time_waited / 100),2)) sum_secs
from
        sys.v_$system_event
where
        event not in
        ('lock element cleanup',
        'pmon timer',
        'rdbms ipc message',
        'smon timer',
        'SQL*Net message from client',
        'SQL*Net break/reset to client',
        'SQL*Net message to client',
        'SQL*Net more data to client',
        'dispatcher timer',
        'Null event',
        'parallel query dequeue wait',
        'parallel query idle wait - Slaves',
        'pipe get',
        'PL/SQL lock timer',
        'slave wait',
        'virtual circuit status',
        'WMON goes to sleep') and
        event not like 'DFS%' and
        event not like 'KXFX%')
order by
    2 desc;
```

	EVENT	TOTAL_WAITS	PCT_TOT_WAITS	TIME_WAIT_SEC	PCT_TIME_WAITS	TOTAL_TIMEOUTS	AVG_WAIT_SEC
1	control file parallel write	77154	64.69	67.18	37.74	0	0
2	direct path write	18271	15.32	28.54	16.03	0	0
3	control file sequential read	10531	8.83	24.74	13.9	0	0
4	direct path read	7758	6.5	34.86	19.58	0	0
5	db file sequential read	2627	2.2	5.33	2.99	0	0
6	refresh controlfile command	1401	1.17	10.94	6.15	0	.01
7	log file parallel write	477	.4	.45	.25	1	0
8	log file sync	276	.23	1.4	.79	0	.01
9	db file parallel write	266	.22	1.94	1.09	0	.01
10	file open	156	.13	.99	.56	0	.01
11	db file scattered read	125	.1	.11	.06	0	0
12	latch free	97	.08	1.11	.62	89	.01
13	file identify	47	.04	.18	.1	0	0
14	buffer busy waits	22	.02	.02	.01	0	0
15	library cache pin	21	.02	0	0	0	0
16	LGWR wait for redo copy	9	.01	.03	.02	3	0
17	rdbms ipc reply	7	.01	0	0	0	0
18	log file sequential read	5	0	0	0	0	0
19	log file single write	5	0	0	0	0	0
20	single-task message	5	0	.18	.1	0	.04
21	SQL*Net more data from client	4	0	0	0	0	0
22	reliable message	1	0	0	0	0	0
23	library cache load lock	1	0	0	0	0	0
24	instance state change	1	0	0	0	0	0

Figure 2.1 – Sample output showing system waits

Appendix A in the Oracle Reference Manual contains a listing and description of every current wait event defined in Oracle. DBAs unfamiliar with what each event represents should keep this listing close by as they examine wait-based event metrics. For example, in the above listing, the db file sequential read has the most total wait time of any event.

But, what is a 'db file sequential' read anyway? Database file sequential reads normally indicate index lookup operations or ROWID fetches from a table. If the requested Oracle blocks are not already in memory, the initiating process must wait for them to be read in. Such activity seems to be the main source of contention in the above listing.

After looking at system-level wait activity, a DBA can drill down further to discover which current connections may be responsible for any reported waits that are being observed at the system level. One query that can be used to collect such data is the *sesswaits.sql* script:

sesswaits.sql

```
SELECT
      b.sid,
      decode(b.username,NULL,c.name,b.username) process_name,
      event,
      a.total_waits,
      round((a.time_waited / 100),2)
      time_wait_sec,a.total_timeouts,
      round((average_wait / 100),2)
      average_wait_sec,
      round((a.max_wait / 100),2) max_wait_sec
   FROM
      sys.v_$session_event a,
      sys.v_$session b,
      sys.v_$bgprocess c
   WHERE
         event NOT IN
            ('lock element cleanup',
            'pmon timer',
            'rdbms ipc message',
            'smon timer',
            'SQL*Net message from client',
            'SQL*Net break/reset to client',
            'SQL*Net message to client',
```

```
                'SQL*Net more data to client',
                'dispatcher timer',
                'Null event',
                'parallel query dequeue wait',
                'parallel query idle wait - Slaves',
                'pipe get',
                'PL/SQL lock timer',
                'slave wait',
                'virtual circuit status',
                'WMON goes to sleep'
                )
        and event NOT LIKE 'DFS%'
        and event NOT LIKE 'KXFX%'
        and a.sid = b.sid
        and b.paddr = c.paddr (+)
order by
        4 desc;
```

	SID	PROCESS_NAME	EVENT	TOTAL_WAITS	TIME_WAIT_SEC	TOTAL_TIMEOUTS	AVERAGE_WAIT_SEC	MAX_WAIT_SEC
1	4	CKPT	control file parallel write	729	8.77	0	.01	.86
2	11	SYS	control file sequential read	262	2.54	0	.01	.14
3	4	CKPT	control file sequential read	228	10.31	0	.05	.23
4	5	SMON	db file scattered read	124	13.08	0	.11	.22
5	9	SCHED	db file sequential read	111	8.84	0	.08	.19
6	11	SYS	db file sequential read	73	3.69	0	.05	.15
7	3	LGWR	log file parallel write	69	1.92	64	.03	.13
8	5	SMON	db file sequential read	68	6.13	0	.09	.19
9	2	DBW0	control file sequential read	35	1.74	0	.05	.25
10	3	LGWR	control file sequential read	30	1.91	0	.06	.16
11	2	DBW0	direct path read	18	.22	0	.01	.15
12	2	DBW0	db file parallel write	16	.22	16	.01	.08
13	3	LGWR	control file parallel write	14	1.43	0	.1	.26
14	3	LGWR	direct path read	9	0	0	0	0
15	8	SYS	db file sequential read	8	.25	0	.03	.08
16	3	LGWR	direct path write	8	.17	0	.02	.17
17	3	LGWR	log file single write	7	.33	0	.05	.07
18	3	LGWR	log file sequential read	6	.22	0	.04	.07
19	9	SCHED	log file sync	3	.08	0	.03	.03
20	11	SYS	library cache pin	3	.12	0	.04	.12
21	2	DBW0	async disk IO	2	.22	0	.11	.15
22	3	LGWR	async disk IO	2	.17	0	.09	.17
23	11	SYS	buffer busy waits	1	.01	0	.01	.01
24	6	RECO	db file sequential read	1	.12	0	.12	.12

Figure 2.2 – Sample historical wait output at the session level

Such a query, for example, could indicate the Oracle
processes responsible for most of the db file sequential
waits that were reported in the global system overview
query. Like the system-level query, the above query shows
cumulative wait statistics for each session since it has been
connected (all data for that session is lost once it
disconnects from the database).

A final level of detail can be obtained by checking for any
active Oracle processes that are currently waiting. One
query that can be used to uncover such data is the
csesswaits.sql script:

---

csesswaits.sql

```
SELECT
        a.sid,
        decode(b.username,NULL,c.name,b.username) process_name,
        a.event,
        a.seconds_in_wait,
        a.wait_time,
        a.state,
        a.p1text,
        a.p1,
        a.p1raw,
        a.p2text,
        a.p2,
        a.p2raw,
        a.p3text,
        a.p3,
        a.p3raw
   FROM
        sys.v_$session_wait a,
        sys.v_$session b,
        sys.v_$bgprocess c
   WHERE
        event NOT IN
          ('lock element cleanup',
          'pmon timer',
          'rdbms ipc message',
          'smon timer',
          'SQL*Net message from client',
          'SQL*Net break/reset to client',
          'SQL*Net message to client',
          'SQL*Net more data to client',
          'dispatcher timer',
          'Null event',
          'parallel query dequeue wait',
          'parallel query idle wait - Slaves',
          'pipe get',
          'PL/SQL lock timer',
          'slave wait',
          'virtual circuit status',
          'WMON goes to sleep'
          )
   and event NOT LIKE 'DFS%'
   and event NOT LIKE 'KXFX%'
   and a.sid = b.sid
   and b.paddr = c.paddr (+)
order by
        4 desc;
```

	SID	PROCESS_NAME	EVENT	SECONDS_IN_WAIT	WAIT_TIME	STATE	P1TEXT	P1	P1RAW	P2TEXT	P2	P2RAW	P3TEXT	P3	P3RAW
1	10	ERADMIN	enqueue	3	0	WAITING	name|mode	1415053318	54580006	id1	524312	00080018	id2	31373	00007A8D

Figure 2.3 – Output showing a session currently waiting on a resource

If a DBA notices a current process, for example, in a db file sequential read wait, data contained in the parameter columns of the above query (p1text, p1, etc.) can be used to locate the exact file and block of the object being used by Oracle to satisfy the end user's request.

If you find enqueue waits present when you examine the output of current session waits, you can use the *objwait.sql* script to find which object and datafile are causing the holdup:

objwaits.sql

```
select
      sid,
      username,
      machine,
      program,
      b.owner,
      b.object_type,
      b.object_name,
      c.file_name
from  sys.v_$session a,
      sys.dba_objects b,
      sys.dba_data_files c
where a.row_wait_obj# > 0 and
      a.row_wait_obj# = b.object_id and
      a.row_wait_file# = c.file_id
order by sid
```

	SID	USERNAME	MACHINE	PROGRAM	OWNER	OBJECT_TYPE	OBJECT_NAME	FILE_NAME
1	10	ERADMIN	MSHOME\ROBINS	sqlplusw.exe	ERADMIN	TABLE	ADMISSION_TEST	C:\ORACLE\ORA90\RMSD\USERS01.DBF

Figure 2.4 – Uncovering the objects and datafiles involved in an enqueue wait

When using bottleneck analysis, a DBA cannot rely *only* on the information contained in the wait event views that Oracle provides. For example, an object may attempt to extend into another extent of space in a tablespace and yet, be denied if no such free space exists.

Such a failure will not be reflected in any wait event but still represents a very real bottleneck to the database. In the same way that a DBA cannot depend on only a few ratios to properly carry out ratio-based performance analysis; an administrator must include several statistical metrics in their overall bottleneck analysis framework to obtain an accurate performance-risk assessment.

For example, in the aforementioned object extension failure, the DBA would want to include a query in his bottleneck analysis framework that returns a count of any object that has reached (or better yet, approaches) its maximum extent limit or is housed in a tablespace with insufficient free space to accommodate its next extent.

Now that we have reviewed each method, let's examine an effective approach that combines bottleneck and ratio analysis techniques.

Combining Bottleneck and Ratio Analysis

To provide the best possible coverage for a database, a DBA should utilize both ratio-based and bottleneck analysis in their performance-monitoring toolkit. While there are many ways to accomplish this, one approach is to categorize each area of performance interest, and then list out the metrics that should be used for both ratio-based and bottleneck analysis.

Realize that some ratio-based metrics can be represented as bottleneck metrics and vice-versa (for example, while a ratio could be used to indicate how full an Oracle archive log destination has become, such a measure could also be used as a bottleneck metric that represents an approaching space-related blockage), and some metrics can overlap categories.

To summarize the strength and weakness of each approach:

Ratio-based analysis:

- Offers a quick approach to getting a bird's eye view of performance metrics.

- Scales fairly easily when monitoring many databases.

- Covers areas overlooked by bottleneck analysis.

- Can be misleading if performed incorrectly (using cumulative instead of delta statistics), and must be interpreted in light of each database's distinct 'personality'.

Bottleneck analysis:

- Pinpoints showstopper events better than ratio-based analysis.

- Can provide deeper insight into where a database is spending its time.

- Must utilize other metrics, besides Oracle wait events.

- Can miss some insightful statistics only found by using ratio-based analysis.

There are, of course, many ways to categorize each area of performance in a database, and even more variations of which metrics to include for each area and style of performance-measurement practice. However, one generic arrangement could be the following:

Performance Area: Memory

Ratio-Based Metrics	Bottleneck-Based Metrics
Buffer Cache Hit Ratio	Buffer Busy
Data Dictionary Cache Hit Ratio	Enqueue Waits
	Free Buffer Waits
Free Shared Pool Percent	Latch Free Waits
Library Cache Hit Ratio	Library Cache Pin Waits
Memory/Disk Sort Ratio	Library Cache Load Lock
Parse/Execute Ratio	Waits
Leading Memory Session	Log Buffer Space Waits
Percentage	Library Object Reloads Count
	Redo Log Space Waits
	Redo Log Space Wait Time

Table 2.1 – Ratio-Based Metrics to Bottleneck-Based Metrics

Note how the various metrics complement one another to form a near-complete picture of memory activity.

Performance Area: I/O

Ratio-Based Metrics	Bottleneck-Based Metrics
Buffer Cache Hit Ratio Chained Table Access Ratio Index/Table Scan Access Ratio Leading I/O Session Percentage Leading CPU Session Percentage	Control File Parallel Write Waits Control File Sequential Read Waits DB File Parallel Read Waits DB File Parallel Write Waits DB File Single Write Waits DB File Scattered Read Waits DB File Sequential Read Waits Direct Path Read Waits Direct Path Write Waits Log File Sequential Read Waits Log File Parallel Write Waits Log File Sync Waits Sort Segment Request Waits Write Complete Waits

Table 2.2 – Performance Area I/O

Notice in the above lists how wait events reveal more in the area of I/O analysis than in most other areas.

Performance Area: Space

Ratio-Based Metrics	Bottleneck-Based Metrics
Archive Log Destination Free Space Percent	Archive Log Destination Full
Individual Tablespace Free Space Percent	Autoextend Datafiles Near/At Maximum Extend Limit
Individual Tablespace Fragmentation Ratio	Objects Near/At Maximum Extent Count
Redo Log Space Wastage Ratio	Objects Near/At Free Space Extend Failure
Redo Log Switch Ratio	Offline Tablespace Count
Total Free Space Ratio	Log File Switch Wait

Table 2.3 – Performance Area: Space

Notice how bottleneck analysis would be almost useless in monitoring space if you were only relying on wait events.

Performance Area: Objects

Ratio-Based Metrics	Bottleneck-Based Metrics
Active Rollback Ratio	Chained Table Count
Blocking Lock Ratio	Free List Waits
Chained Row Fetch Ratio	Enqueue Waits
Invalid Object Percentage	Objects Near/At Maximum Extent Count
Rollback Contention Ratio	Objects Near/At Free Space Extend Failure
	Table High-Water Mark Problem Count
	Tables and Child Indexes in Same Tablespace

Ratio-Based Metrics	Bottleneck-Based Metrics
	Count
	Undo Segment Extension

Table 2.4 – Performance Area: Objects

Notice again, how bottleneck analysis would be almost useless in monitoring objects (like space) if you were only relying on wait events.

Performance Area: User Activity

Ratio-Based Metrics	Bottleneck-Based Metrics
Active Rollback Ratio	Blocked Session Count
Active/Total Session Ratio	Transaction Waits
Blocking Lock Ratio	
CPU/Parse Ratio	
Parse/Execute Ratio	
Rollback/Commit Ratio	

Table 2.5 – Performance Area: User Activity

There are likely many variations of the above ratios and bottleneck metrics, and others that could be included as well, but these categories and listings should serve as a starting place. Nearly all the metrics contained in the above tables can be obtained by using the scripts that are referenced throughout this book.

Now it's time to examine a third technique for investigating database performance – workload analysis.

Workload Analysis

Key ratios help a person get a global perspective on database activity and bottleneck analysis assists the DBA by offering insight into things that are holding up user activity and throughput. But, another technique is necessary if a database professional is to really get a handle on what is occurring inside a badly performing database.

Workload analysis involves the investigation of two critical areas of a database's performance:

- Session resource consumption and activity
- SQL execution

Without looking at these two key performance categories, a DBA will miss much of what could be responsible for perceived performance problems.

Session Resource Consumption

When performance on a database takes a sudden nosedive, it is not uncommon to find one or two sessions that are causing the bulk of the workload. This can be easily accomplished by viewing session metadata coupled with resource consumption and statistical execution statistics.

Chapter seven of this book goes into great detail on how to locate problem sessions on a system and drill down into the heart of what they are doing and the amount of resources they are using. Being able to effectively do this will enable you to have the first key to the workload analysis puzzle.

SQL Execution

Needless to say, a DBA needs to be able to pinpoint resource-intensive SQL code that is causing undo strain on a database. Understanding current and historical SQL execution patterns will enable you to have the second set of data necessary to properly perform workload analysis.

Chapter eight of this book covers techniques and provides scripts to help you interrogate Oracle and find SQL calls that might require optimization. You will likely find that optimizing SQL code will produce some of the best performance-enhancing boosts available for a database.

Keep in mind that while locating SQL calls that are racking up expensive statistics is not hard, the actual art of optimizing SQL can be quite difficult. While there are third party software products that can help in rewriting SQL queries, you won't find one that will tell you that a particular SQL statement should not be executed.

Only by understanding a particular application's needs can this be accomplished. Removing SQL 'waste' in a database can produce dramatic results as, believe it or not, sometimes the best SQL query is the one you *don't* execute.

Conclusion

Using a singular diagnostic approach to database performance analysis may, under the right conditions, result in pinpointing a database slowdown, but a more holistic approach is to utilize metrics and collection methods from both ratio-based and bottleneck analysis, as well as techniques found in workload analysis. As with investing in the stock market, a person might not be right every time, but they can limit most losses by staying true to a combined and proven methodology.

The main points to keep in mind with respect to material contained in this chapter are:

- When practiced correctly, ratio-based analysis is still a viable technique to use when analyzing database performance.

- Bottleneck analysis is indeed a powerful method for reviewing a database's performance; however, it must be extended to include more metrics than just Oracle wait events.

- Workload analysis offers critical insight into a database's performance puzzle by bubbling to the forefront sessions and SQL code that is responsible for the bulk of system activity

- Combining ratio-based, bottleneck, and workload analysis techniques yields a solid package that should equip you to handle almost every performance-tuning situation.

The next chapter will look at how you can pinpoint the sessions in your database that are not only causing the most bottlenecks but are using the majority of the database's resources and are, in turn, making everyone else's life miserable.

Chapter 3

Correcting Foundational Flaws

Perhaps one of the largest benefits to working as a consultant is to witness great examples of 'how not to do it.' One engagement that comes to mind involved a client who was having a terrible problem with query response time, from both his custom-built GUI and ad-hoc reporting tools.

The technical scenario was an Oracle database that resided on an IBM AIX UNIX server with Microsoft Windows© clients connecting to it. The response time to receive a query result could top an hour or more for some reports. Clearly, something had to change.

The first thing done was to run a complete set of database diagnostics, as well as UNIX diagnostics, and analyze the results. A number of definite problems were found in both the placement of database files and heavy database fragmentation, which no doubt contributed to the overall response time problem.

Still, something else had to be the main culprit for such a pronounced lag in response time. One of the typical reports that had been requested was reviewed in detail. The report included a fairly complex query that joined a number of database views. On the surface, nothing appeared wildly out of place. It was only upon closer examination of the underlying views that the light began to dawn.

The first view used in the report was simply amazing. It involved a selection of 43 columns that joined *33* tables and had a join predicate that contained not less than *28 outer joins*. And remember, this was just *one* view involved with the report.

The important point in this example is that even if you adhere to every database tuning guideline for building your system, you will still fail miserably if your physical database design is wrong. Obviously, the database described above was suffering from a red-hot case of extreme normalization. Instead of recognizing and addressing their bad design, the project leaders had hoped to see some quick tuning magic that would set things right.

Sadly, they were informed that it would not be that easy. Isn't it funny that to help improve performance, many turn to high-paid database consultants and spend tens of thousands of dollars on database performance monitors that track thousands of statistics, only to be left shaking their head at a system that crawls along? As an Oracle database professional, the one thing you must always keep in the back of your mind when examining a database's performance is the actual physical design.

This chapter addresses the critical importance of database design and demonstrates how some of the problems you may be having with your database right now are the result of an improper physical setup.

Why is Physical Design Overlooked?

When troubleshooting performance problems, why do database professionals overlook the physical database design? The primary reason is that most DBAs have been taught that bad SQL or insufficient resources (hardware, memory, etc.) are usually the main culprits for poor database performance. It is easier to hunt for bad SQL and throw hardware at a slow-running database than interrogate a database's physical design for two main reasons:

- A proper physical design is difficult to construct correctly

- A proper physical design takes time (and sometimes lots of it)

When data modelers begin creating a non-RDBMS specific database design, the model is labeled a 'logical' design. The modelers work hard at 'normalization', where they ensure the model is relationally accurate (all entities have primary keys; all attributes in an entity depend on the primary key, etc.). That design is then oftentimes turned over to DBAs to create a 'physical' design, which is a specifically targeted model for a particular RDBMS, like Oracle.

Designing a high performance database is complicated work. It takes skill and experience to get a design that runs like greased lightning. But sadly, experienced database personnel are at a premium these days, so junior or completely green IT workers are called upon to design and build a database.

The mindset of needing a staff of experienced logical data modelers was all but thrown out in the early nineties, when CASE tools that promised everything under the sun cracked under the strain of real world business models. Since many CASE tools failed to deliver what they had promised, and because many of these tools stressed logical design as the necessary forerunner of a good system, logical design was discounted with respect to its importance.

Corporations had endured so many projects that never got off the drawing board that RAD (Rapid Application Development) became the accepted mode of development. The end result was - and still is - that logical and physical design is not taken nearly as seriously in overall system development as it should.

The second reason quality designs are overlooked when the topic of performance is discussed is that a lot of up-front time is needed to create a good design. And, time is not what a lot of companies have these days. The application lifecycle has never been shorter in corporations than it is right now.

Projects that would have taken years to complete just five years ago are being thrown up in six months or less. Obviously, to accomplish such a feat requires one of two things: (1) superior personnel using state-of-the art software tools or (2) the elimination of necessary tasks from the application construction equation.

Usually, one of the first compromises is the abandonment of the database logical design phase. The reason for this is that the project leaders believe that all will be well if the database is designed beside the application code. Instead of sitting down and intelligently laying out the necessary components and objects of a database, the database structure is built in the development phase alongside the code base used to run the application. The end result is a design that never had a chance to succeed.

Instead of concentrating on good physical database design, database professionals look to other methods to enhance performance. However, when they do, they risk missing the boat entirely and could end up dazed and confused with a database that simply will not perform.

The Number One Performance Myth

Whether it's in the realm of database technology or any other discipline, some maxims are whispered around the campfire so much that they are taken for gospel on face value and never questioned, especially when supposed "experts" mouth the words. Such is the case with a database performance myth that has been around for as long as most can remember. It goes something like this:

"Eighty percent of a database's overall performance is derived from the code that is written against it."

This is a complete untruth, or at the very least, an overestimation of the impact that properly written SQL code has against a running physical database. Good coding practices definitely count (often heavily) toward the success of any database application, but to state affirmatively that they make a contribution of over two-thirds is a stretch.

The reason this proverb cannot pass the reality test is that it is stated independently of what good or bad code can do in the face of poor physical design. The real world case that opened this chapter is a shining example of how wrong this adage is.

The physical design constrains all code - good or bad - and has the capability to turn even the best written SQL into molasses.

After all, how can a SQL developer obtain unique key index access unless the physical index has been created and is in place?

How can a database coder scan only the parts of a table that they need unless that table has been partitioned to accommodate such a request? Only when a solid physical design is put in place - a design that fits the application like a glove - can SQL code really take off and make for some impressive response times. But, good design comes first.

The Link between Performance Monitoring and Physical Design

Every database professional wants to be thought of as an expert in database tuning. The consultants that make the most money out in the field are the ones who can miraculously transform a sluggish, wheezing database into one that runs fast and efficiently. The books that fly off the shelf in the technical bookstores are the ones that promise secret hidden tips on accelerating the performance of database systems.

A good DBA covets his complicated SQL scripts that dig into the heart of a database's internals and regurgitate mountains of difficult-to-interpret statistics. But, do those down-in-the-database DBAs really know what to do with all the information produced through performance monitors and SQL scripts? How does a DBA effectively monitor a database for performance and make a difference in the response time and the user's experience?

The key to understanding the discipline of performance monitoring is this: *When you monitor a database for performance, you are really validating your physical design implementation.* If the performance monitor you choose to use is blasting you with flashing lights, alarm bells, and pager alerts, it is probably because your physical design is failing.

If all is quiet on the scene with your performance monitor, then your physical design is likely a current success. It really is *almost* as simple as that.

To be sure, there are performance situations that really are not impacted by the physical design directly. Lock contention, for example, is mostly an application or coding issue. But on a grand scale, your performance monitoring output speaks volumes on your talents as a database designer.

Do you have I/O contention problems in your database? Then, you likely did not segment the tables, indexes, and storage structures properly in your physical design. Are you observing too many long table scans in your database? Chances are you did not adhere to the proper indexing or partitioning strategy.

Are you experiencing out-of-space headaches with either your storage structures or objects? It is a good bet you did not size your database properly in your initial physical design.

The tragic thing is that much of today's mindset dismisses the idea that altering and improving a database's physical design will yield the largest possible performance benefit.

Part of the reason for this is that modifying the design of a physical database, especially one that is currently in production, is no easy task and oftentimes requires healthy amounts of off-hours work by the administrator. So instead, many take the quick fix approach to performance problems, which mean throwing hardware at the situation in most cases. We have three choices:

- The server box itself is upgraded.
- More processors are introduced to the mix.
- A decent amount of RAM is added.

In the short term, things appear to get better, and if the database is relatively static in nature, things may remain that way. But, if the database is dynamic and the data/user load continues to grow, the problem will return.

The reason for this is a foundational one. If the foundation is flawed, then the house needs to be put in order at that level before anything else is done. But, performance monitoring and problem resolution today often is not handled that way. It is like a homeowner discovering that his or her house has a cracked foundation, adding a new coat of paint to cover up the cracks, and declaring that all is well.

Even worse, the homeowner could attempt to add on to their home in hopes of improving the value or appeal.

But, let's face it; with a cracked foundation, who will buy it? The same thing holds true for adding more hardware onto a poorly designed database. You may throw more RAM, etc., at a badly performing database, and for a while, those performance cracks are covered up.

But over time, as more data and users are added, those foundational cracks will reappear and must be dealt with yet again. Regardless of the effort involved, it is much better to attack the foundation problem in order to correct the problems permanently.

As an example, a database administrator who still practices ratio-based analysis may use his or her performance monitor to find that the data buffer cache hit ratio is far below acceptable levels (typically 80% or less). The DBA may erroneously conclude from the situation that more RAM is needed or that the buffer cache should be enlarged to improve performance.

But what if the problem instead, stems from the fact that too many long table scans are occurring? Most RDBMSs will quickly recycle the data obtained from large table scan operations to keep stale data out of the cache. To be sure, the problem could be a coding problem where developers are not using the right indexes in the SQL predicates.

Or, more likely, the database may not have the correct indexes in place to assist the code in avoiding the many long table scans. If this physical design flaw can be correctly identified, then no extra RAM may be needed.

What about the link between availability and design? According to Oracle Corporation's own studies of client downtime, the largest percentage, *up to 36%*, are design-related issues. If you have not been very serious about your database design until now, consider this your wake-up call.

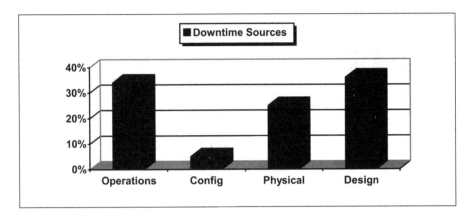

Figure 3.1 - Downtime statistics provide by Oracle Corporation

Making the Biggest Performance Impact

If this chapter has convinced you that proper physical design should be your number one performance goal as a database administrator, then it is time to get serious about how you manage your physical design lifecycle.

So, how do you get started in making a noticeable difference in the physical designs of the databases currently under your care and those you are destined to encounter and/or build in the future?

The first step to take is a mental one and involves making the commitment to pay more attention to excellent physical design. It should be mentioned that all project management personnel need to make this same commitment, as the effort required to guarantee a solid physical design foundation will take more up-front resources. But, make no mistake; to say that it is time well spent is an understatement.

The next step involves education of the database designer. Of course, the best way to become a design guru is to put time in the trenches and work with every style of database: heavy OLTP, data warehousing, and cross-platform data mart designs. You will learn very quickly which designs stand and which physical foundations crack when you go up against heavy-duty web-based and mega-user systems. Of course, there are also a variety of good educational classes and books on the subject of physical design to aid in the learning process.

Creating robust, efficient physical designs can be difficult and intricate work. You will need to arm yourself with some serious power tools that have the capability to slice through the difficulties involved in building and retrofitting complex physical database designs. Long gone are the days when a DBA or modeler could handle most of their work with a SQL query interface and a drawing tool. Today, relational databases are just too robust and contain too many complexities for such primitive aids.

At a minimum, you will need two things flanking both ends of your arsenal: a serious data modeling tool and a robust performance-monitoring product. It has already been established that performance monitoring is really the validation of a database's physical design. When foundational cracks are identified with the monitor, you will need a high-quality design tool to aid in rectifying the situation.

For those physical DBAs who do not like to use data modeling tools, two other software products will be needed: a feature-rich database administration tool and a change control product. The database administration tool will be used to create new objects for a database, as well as modify properties of existing objects. This tool is normally used in an ad-hoc manner and is great for graphically redesigning a database in real-time mode.

The change control product is a different animal. If you will not use a data modeling tool to capture and version control the designs of your databases, then you will need another method for protecting designs that are in place and working. Having such "snapshot backups" of your database's schemas will prove invaluable when disaster strikes.

A seasoned DBA, who was managing a large packaged financial application, once learned the value of a change control tool. She had to make a complex change to one of the database's critical tables and had thought she had built the right script to do the job. Unfortunately, she did not have everything in place, and when she ran her change job, she ended up losing a number of important indexes that existed on the table.

Worse yet, since her table and data looked okay, she thought all was well and did not know she had lost the necessary indexes. The next day, many parts of the application slowed down to a snail's pace as queries that used to complete in an instant were now taking forever.

The changed table was identified as the source of the problem, but while the DBA discovered that the table now had no indexes, she did not know which columns had been indexed (something not uncommon in huge financial applications). Through trial and error, she was able to get her indexing scheme back in place, but not before a lot of time had been lost.

This is one case where a good change control tool can save you. Nearly every good tool in this category offers a synchronization feature that allows a DBA to compare an up-and-running database with a saved snapshot of that database's object definitions. Once differences are identified, a click of the mouse can restore any missing objects.

But, a change control tool can also help you in your physical design iterations. By periodically capturing changes you make to the physical design of your database, you can learn what worked and what did not. And, if you make an "oops" and actually cause more harm than good, you can instruct your change control tool to automatically put things back to the way they were.

Now, if your company does not have the budget to purchase such a tool, you may be able to get by with taking full Oracle exports on a periodic basis with the ROWS parameter set to NO and backing up the export dump files. Doing exports in this manner will capture the DDL for all structures in the database without backing up the actual data. By doing exports in this way, you can build a basic change control process where your table structures, indexes, procedures, etc., are protected in such a way that you can, in an emergency, restore only certain object definitions that have accidentally been dropped.

However, there are drawbacks to using this approach because some objects (like procedures, packages, etc.) cannot be easily restored, and object definition changes cannot be as easily fixed as they can with a smart change control tool. However, it might be better than having no change control process at all.

Spotting Physical Design Flaws

Once you have your database design arsenal in place, you can begin the work of building correct physical designs from scratch and managing the physical design lifecycle once a system goes into production. But, how do you quickly spot physical design flaws in an up-and-running database?

It definitely takes a trained eye to uncover the root cause of identified performance problems, but the table below will help get you started. It lists just a few of the most common database performance problems and the possible physical design gremlins that could be the culprit in an Oracle database.

Performance Category	Performance Problem	Possible Design Cause
Memory	Poor Data Buffer Cache Hit Ratio	• Too many long table scans – invalid indexing scheme

Performance Category	Performance Problem	Possible Design Cause
		• Not enough RAM devoted to buffer cache memory area • Invalid object placement using Oracle's KEEP and RECYCLE buffer caches • Not keeping small lookup tables in cache using CACHE table parameter
	Poor Memory/Disk Sort Ratio	• Not presorting data when possible
Contention	Redo log waits	• Incorrect sizing of Oracle redo logs • Insufficient memory allocated to log buffer area
	Free list waits	• Not enough free lists assigned to tables • Not using Oracle9i's auto segment management
	Rollback waits	• Insufficient number of rollback segments • Not using Oracle9i's

Performance Category	Performance Problem	Possible Design Cause
		auto-UNDO management
I/O	Identified disk contention	• Not separating tables and accompanying indexes into different tablespaces on different physical drives
	Slow access to system information	• Not placing SYSTEM tablespace on little accessed physical drive
	Slow disk sorts	• Placing tablespace used for disk sort activity on RAID5 drive or heavily accessed physical volume
	Abnormally high physical I/O	• Too many long table scans – invalid indexing scheme • Not enough RAM devoted to buffer cache memory area • Invalid object placement using Oracle 8's KEEP and RECYCLE buffer caches • Not keeping small lookup tables in cache

Performance Category	Performance Problem	Possible Design Cause
		using CACHE table parameter
Space	Out of space conditions (storage structures)	• Poorly forecasted data volumes in physical design
	Tablespace fragmentation	• Invalid settings for either object space sizes or tablespace object settings (PCTINCREASE, etc.) • Not using locally-managed tablespaces in Oracle8 and above
SQL	Large JOIN queries	• Over normalized database design
Object activity	Chaining in tables	• Incorrect amount of PCTFREE, PCTUSED settings for objects • Too small database block size
	Rollback extension	• Incorrect sizing of rollback segments for given application transaction • Not using Oracle9i's

Performance Category	Performance Problem	Possible Design Cause
		auto-UNDO management
	Many large table scans	• Incorrect indexing scheme
	Object fragmentation	• Incorrect initial sizing • Not using locally-managed tablespaces

Table 3.1 – Performance Problems and Possible Causes

Using a quality performance monitor, you can be quickly led to the performance headaches in your database, and then, using either your intelligent data-modeling tool or the combination of your database administration/change control product, you can remedy the situation.

Fixing foundational flaws in a database is never easy, but perhaps one day the DBA community will be treated to software that gets things right, before the situation turns ugly.

The Dream Software Tool for Design

The ultimate software tool for improving a database's physical design, and therefore, overall performance, has yet to be delivered. It is a product that would place a database's physical design and environment under a microscope and then produce an expertly altered physical design, crafted especially for the given database's needs.

The data modeling tools on the market can help you build a data model, but they cannot tell you how to build the *right* data model, and that is a subtle but huge difference.

Let's take the case of when a designer should use a bitmap index. Every data modeling tool will allow you to design a bitmap index for a table, but they will not stop you from putting a bitmap index on a table where one doesn't belong.

Determine Cardinality

To determine if a bitmap index should be used, the designer first needs to know the correct column cardinality. For those not familiar with a bitmap index, they work in pretty much a reverse fashion from a normal B-Tree index. Most indexes require high cardinality (many distinct values) in the table column to work effectively. Bitmap indexes are designed to work with low cardinality data.

For example, if you have a database that tracks patients admitted to a hospital, you may have a column in an admissions table called INSURED that tracks whether the patient was insured or not, basically a YES/NO column. This would be a terrible choice for a regular B-Tree index, but could definitely qualify for a bitmap index.

Such indexes can be intelligently used where the case permits, such as the situation where many low cardinality columns can be ANDed together for Oracle's bitmap merge execution plan.

Data Volume

The second thing a designer needs to know when putting a bitmap index on a table is data volume. Most any index is useless when it comes to enhancing performance on tables with little data because most relational databases will ignore an index on small tables and instead, cache and scan the table faster than if index access was used.

On the other hand, if millions of rows were present in our hospital admissions table, then a bitmap index could really prove useful.

Frequency of Update

The third thing a designer needs to know when deciding if a bitmap index will be necessary is whether data modifications occur at frequent levels for the table. Bitmap indexes are notorious for causing performance slowdowns on tables with high DML activity.

Demonstrating the proof of this concept, a DBA once inherited a database that was extremely critical, both in terms of company visibility and bottom line impact. Complaints began to quickly surface in regard to the database's performance, and while many of the normal performance statistics looked good, there seemed to be a bottleneck whenever an OLTP transaction passed through the system.

The DBA quickly traced the problem to the hub table in the database - nearly every transaction passed into and out of this one table. The designer who preceded the DBA had chosen to place *eight* bitmap indexes on this table that was the object of much DML activity in the system. This design decision violated nearly every rule of thumb with respect to bitmap indexes.

Removing all the bitmap indexes produced an end result like the parting of the Red Sea. Response time throughout the system was immediately restored to more than acceptable measures.
The final and perhaps most important consideration for deciding if a bitmap index is right for the table, is the use of user access patterns.

In other words, will the index be *used* at all? If no one asks the question, "How many insured patients were admitted this month?" in a SQL query, the bitmap index placed on the INSURED column in the hospital admissions table is basically useless.

All four points of whether to use a bitmap index on a table column count must be weighed when it comes down to physical design time. The only problem is that a Data Modeler or DBA may not have all the facts needed to make a correct decision before the system goes live. Or, perhaps the designer simply is not privy to the knowledge needed to make the right choice about index placement.

Here is where the dream tool comes into play. First, a data/work load must be imposed on the database to mimic what is to come, with respect to user traffic, user requests, and data volume. If a load-testing tool can be used before a system goes into production to do this – great. Otherwise, a manual user-driven office environment model must be put in place.

In any event, once such a load exists, the yet-to-be-invented tool interrogates the database and captures data volumes, object statistics, and user request patterns. Using this information, the tool then digests the information and constructs a physical design model that fits the system perfectly.

All necessary indexes are present, physical storage placements are correctly in place, and all objects that desperately need denormalizing are reconstructed. The tool would basically tell the designer that this is how your data model should have looked in the beginning.

Until such a product comes along, using a combination of modeling and performance-monitoring tools will be the de facto method for ensuring high performance physical database designs.

Conclusion

So, what was done to fix the slow-running database described at the beginning of this chapter? First, the over-normalization of the database was pointed out to the database modelers and DBAs. Unfortunately, they were not agreeable to working on the design to make things run better. So instead, a small data-mart was created from the transactional database that the end users could work against to build the reports they needed.

A small extract-transform-load (ETL) routine was also written and fronted with an easy to use GUI that the users could run whenever they liked to refresh the data-mart's contents. While their reports had run for over an hour before, the entire ETL process and report process now crossed the finish line in under seven minutes.

And if the ETL routine did not need to be run, the actual report creation could be accomplished in about two minutes. A better design, suited to the end users needs, was just the ticket to make things right.

The main points of this chapter to remember include:

- Never compromise a project by neglecting the database's physical design phase

- Understand that much of a database's performance comes from its physical design foundation

- When troubleshooting system performance, keep an eye on indicators that signal a problem with the overall database physical design

One critical aspect of a physical design is the creation and placement of storage structures and the storage characteristics of the database objects. The next chapter will look at how to design your storage objects so that they work for you instead of against you.

Chapter 4

Optimizing Storage

If you could track what has historically caused a DBA's pager or cell phone to summon its owner back to work, it would be a fair bet to say that a leading cause would be storage-related problems. However, the good news is that this does not have to be the case any longer.

Using many of the new features Oracle has added to its flagship database, a DBA can intelligently take proactive steps to ensure that most space problems become a thing of the past. And, even when space problems do arise, most can be quickly diagnosed and remedied by following a few simple steps.

This chapter takes a look at the impact of storage on the overall performance of your database and provides techniques and scripts to aid you in the task of optimizing your storage structures. The questions that will be answered in this chapter include:

- How does storage contribute or detract from a database's performance?

- What storage design decisions should you make up front to help performance?

- How can you intelligently reduce database downtime by optimizing your storage?

- What critical storage headaches should you take pains to avoid?

- How can you detect and resolve the silent storage killers that are robbing your database of its optimum performance?

The Contribution of Storage to Performance

A number of years ago, one of the most visible database-driven systems at a large energy company began to hang. Rebooting the system (the first silver bullet tried by many a systems professional) did not help. It also did not matter whether one or a hundred users attempted to log on - the application and database moved at a snail's pace.

Nothing had changed at the hardware level, and all server diagnostics signaled that everything was in tiptop shape. No changes had been made at the database level either – all the database settings that had run what had previously been a fast system, remained constant. What could have happened to cause such a dramatic shift in performance?

Only when the DBA began to examine what was going on behind the scenes, did the performance gremlin come to light. It seemed that the application made heavy use of the Oracle job queues.

For some reason, the application that was used to create new jobs in the queues went haywire and inserted tens of thousands of jobs into the job queue. The problem was quickly found on the application side, and all the erroneous jobs were deleted.

Now, however, whenever the job queue system table was referenced (and it was referenced every 10 seconds), the system seemed to grind to a halt. The DBA discovered that the job queue table contained only three rows in it, but the highwater mark of the table (the last block Oracle will read when a scan occurs) was thousands of blocks high.

The delete of all the mistakenly submitted jobs may have removed the actual jobs, but Oracle thought that the system table still contained lots of data because of the highwater mark setting (more on this subject later).

To rectify the situation, the DBA entered a *truncate* for the system table, which reset the table's highwater mark. Once this was done, the database completely returned to normal. In this case, a storage-related problem for a table had brought the entire database to an absolute standstill.

While DBAs focus on memory settings and tuning SQL, they oftentimes forget just how dangerous and insidious storage problems can be. This is not a good mindset because storage headaches can play a major role in wrecking an otherwise well-running database.

Storage problems generally take one of two forms:

- The 'hit-the-wall' variety that can bring things to a complete standstill.

- The 'performance vampire' kind that slowly drains the performance of a database over time.

-

Storage problems have the capability to bring the curtain down on a database very quickly. If you doubt this is true, just ask any DBA how well their database runs when the archive log destination runs out of free space. But, storage problems can also silently work behind the scenes to slowly but surely rob a database of its performance.

For example, a hub table in a busy database may be accessed very quickly when an application is first given life, but over time, if it develops a heavy migrated row problem, it can cause things to run very differently.

The rest of this chapter will discuss how you can avoid both types of these storage traps.

Storage Design Considerations

Chapter two discussed how important the physical design of your database is with respect to performance. Part of any physical design is the planning that goes into the creation of the actual storage structures, as well as the storage properties of your database objects.

Your storage planning should actually be done on three different levels:

- The hardware/disk level

- The storage structure level

- The object level

Hardware/Disk Planning

A DBA should take into account everything that occurs on a database server and not only the activity and needs of the actual database. For example, the operating system will have storage needs in addition to the database, as might any application that is placed on the machine (although this should be avoided if at all possible).

The bottom line is that a DBA should look at the server disk layout and try to map out a strategy that promotes a fast database. What are some things that should be taken into consideration? At a minimum, the following items must be closely examined:

Storage/disk Management Mechanisms

This generally involves whether to use RAID (redundant array of inexpensive disks) technology or JBOD (just a bunch of disks). Complicating the decision on what type of RAID to use is that many of the hardware vendors offer 'smart' storage technology that promises to give the DBA the best of both possible worlds.

For example, most DBAs know that write-intensive storage structures should not be placed on a RAID5 setup because of the write penalty that RAID5 imposes. Therefore, a smart DBA would try and place all their rollback structures, online redo logs, temporary tablespaces, and other write-intensive objects on non-RAID5 devices, with the best situation normally being RAID0+1.

However, a number of hardware vendors claim to have "auto" or "smart" RAID storage devices that offer the protection of RAID5 with the write speed of a RAID0 or RAID1 device. The DBA should investigate and test the claims of such devices to see if they actually produce the claimed results.

Database Storage Structure Placement

A DBA hopes to have many different physical devices operating under separate controllers so that everything possible can be done to minimize disk I/O contention, both at the database and operating system levels.

Many DBAs intend to place all operating system software on one device, with the Oracle database software on another device, and then build their database across all the other devices. It is common knowledge that most DBAs desire to stripe their database across multiple devices (for example, put their SYSTEM tablespace on one device, stripe the redo log groups across other devices, etc.), so this will not be discussed in detail. Remember also, do a little capacity planning so that the future space requirements of the database are taken into account as well.

Backup/recovery Needs

Oftentimes, this critical storage component is overlooked, and if it is, it can come back to haunt you in a terrible way. When designing your physical database, you should think about the space requirements for your archive logs (and the multiple destinations that you can now use with Oracle8i and above) and any hot backup or export utility requirements. It is definitely smart to leave ample free space available for these needs, as you may find yourself pigeonholed if you come up short in these areas.

The Coming Physical I/O Crisis

A number of database experts are predicting a coming crisis with respect to database performance and disk I/O.

This prediction has to do with the fact that hard disks are continually increasing in their ability to handle more storage capacity, however the I/O's per second (iops) that these disks can service has not kept pace with their ability to handle more space.

For example, a DBA used to have at their disposal ten or more disks to service the storage needs of a 500GB database. But now, storage vendors can offer IT managers the ability to store that much data on only two disks. Such a proposal is not only attractive to IT management, but it often appeals to system administrators as well because fewer disks mean less work (normally) and maintenance.

However, such a situation can place a stranglehold on the DBA's database because the number of iops that such a disk configuration can handle is far below the iops capability of the previous ten disks.

Storage is typically priced by capacity, and not by iops, so database gurus are sounding the alarm for all DBAs to hear: make sure your voice is heard when the storage configuration of your database server is being decided. If you don't, you may find your database robbed of its performance because of poor disk purchasing decisions.

Storage Structure Planning

This type of planning generally involves the creation and placement of your tablespaces. As was already mentioned above, you want to avoid disk I/O contention where possible, so having several disks available to plot out the map of your database is good.

There are many techniques that DBAs can employ to design their actual physical database structure and a number of good papers that can guide you (such as Oracle's OFA architecture guidelines, etc.).

A very generic Oracle database layout would be:

- **Disk 1** – SYSTEM tablespace

- **Disk 2-4** – Multiplexed online redo logs (not RAID5)

- **Disk 5** – UNDO (rollback) tablespace (not RAID5)

- **Disk 6** – Temporary tablespace (not RAID5)

- **Disk 7** – Static table tablespace

- **Disk 8** – Static index tablespace

- **Disk 9** – Dynamic table tablespace

- **Disk 10** – Dynamic index tablespace

Oracle control files may also be sprinkled throughout this layout. Keep in mind, the above is very generic, and each database has different needs. Also, keep in mind that having many datafiles can elongate database checkpoint procedures.

Locally-managed Tablespaces (LMTs)

Beginning with 8i, Oracle began to introduce many new features that helped DBAs plan and manage their storage structures in a more efficient manner. Topping the list are locally-managed tablespaces that first appeared in Oracle8i and are now the recommended practice for storage management in Oracle9i. The other form of tablespace extent management, *dictionary-managed* tablespaces, had been the norm in Oracle until 8i came along.

In a locally-managed tablespace, space management tasks are handled by bitmaps stored within the tablespace itself. A bitmap is used to keep track of the block status in each datafile, whether they are free or used. Each bit in the bitmap maps to a block or a group of blocks in the datafile.

When extents are allocated or released (marked free), Oracle modifies the bitmap values to show the new status of each block. Part of the good news is that these changes do not generate rollback information because they do not update the system tables in the data dictionary, with the rare exception of cases such as tablespace quota updates. There are a number of benefits that locally-managed tablespaces offer:

- **Less contention** - OLTP systems profit from fewer dictionary concurrency problems because Oracle manages space in the tablespace rather than the data dictionary. Recursive space management calls become a thing of the past. Folks who endure parallel server (or RAC) installations will appreciate this success indicator, as "pinging" between nodes may be substantially reduced

- **No high extent penalty** - Objects can have nearly unlimited numbers of space extents with apparently no performance degradation. Such a feature eliminates the problem of object extent fragmentation outright.

- **Better free space management** - Free space found in datafiles does not have to be coalesced because bitmaps track free space and allocate it much more effectively than dictionary-managed tablespaces. This benefit eliminates the problem of honeycomb fragmentation completely.

- **Efficient space management** - Uniform or system-managed extent sizes are automatically controlled for the database administrator, resulting in a much more efficient space management process. The result is an end to the problem of tablespace bubble fragmentation

Without a doubt, locally-managed tablespaces are a great storage aid for the Oracle DBA. More will be said about them later in this chapter.

Using locally-managed tablespaces in Oracle9i and above enables the DBA to profit from a further feature, automatic segment management (ASM). The traditional form of segment management, free lists, is still maintained, but you owe it to yourself to investigate ASM.

Instead of compiling free lists to document the available space for incoming rows in each block segment, a locally-managed tablespace configured with ASM uses a bitmap. Not only is this new method more efficient than free list management, but you also do not have to fool with the *pctused* property of objects.

Oracle Managed Files (OMF)

Oracle9i has introduced some new features that up the ante for better management and performance of storage structures and have the potential to really make a difference in the database. On the better manageability front, you can

---

make use of Oracle Managed Files (OMF) when creating your database.

For simple databases (or databases using a large RAID design), using OMF eases tablespace and redo log placement because the location of these storage structures is held in Oracle's configuration file (SPFILE). From a storage conservation standpoint, OMF is nice because it will automatically remove any datafiles from the server when a tablespace is dropped. Note that OMF does have its drawbacks, especially for databases that require striping over many physical disks.

Multiple Blocksizes

Another new Oracle9i addition you should be aware of when planning your storage structures is the multiple block size tablespace feature. Prior to Oracle9i, every tablespace assumed the database's block size.

With Oracle9i, a DBA can now create tablespaces that have smaller or larger blocksizes than the database. Why would you want to make use of this feature, and how can it help performance? While many objects in an Oracle database will benefit from the standard 4K or 8K blocksize, there are other objects and structures that benefit from having a large blocksize. Before Oracle9i, you could not mix the two, but now you can. Some objects that benefit from a larger blocksize (16K to 32K) include:

- Most indexes because of the serial nature of index range scans

- Large tables that are the target of full table scans

- Tables with large object (BLOB, CLOB, etc.) data

- Tables with large row sizes that might blossom into chained/migrated rows

- Temporary tablespaces used for sorting

Keep in mind, to utilize the new multi-blocksize feature; you must enable the new memory caches (*db_16k_cache_size, db_32k_cache_size,* etc.) that house the blocks from the different-sized tablespaces.

The Oracle9i Undo Tablespaces

One other new Oracle9i storage feature worth mentioning is the concept of an UNDO tablespace. For years, Oracle DBAs have worked diligently to have the proper rollback management structures in place to handle all the "whoops" activity in their database.

Now, Oracle9i eases this burden by offering automatic management of rollback functions through UNDO tablespaces. UNDO tablespaces can either be created when the database is designed or built later. They are implemented through the *undo_management* configuration parameter.

The idea behind automatic UNDO management is that Oracle controls how many rollback segments are available for use, along with their size. The desired goal is the elimination of rollback waits, extends, and other performance-sapping problems.

Object Planning

When dealing with the storage properties of objects like tables and indexes, the only 'tweakable' items for a long time were the PCTFREE and PCTUSED parameters. Such is not the case any longer, as the Oracle DBA has many more options at his or her disposal.

When planning the storage and placement of your object structures, keep the following points in mind:

- **Use LMTs** - Almost all objects should now be placed into locally-managed tablespaces to avoid the headaches that used to be associated with object-based fragmentation (reaching maximum extent limits, performance degradation due to many extents, etc.).

- **Use multiple blocksizes** - If Oracle9i is being used, then indexes, large tables that are scanned often, tables whose rows have the capability to exceed a small database block size, and LOB tables should be placed into tablespaces with large block sizes (16K – 32K).

- **Separate tables and child indexes** - If distinct, physical drives are being used on the database server, then tables and their child indexes should be physically separated onto different drives.

- **Use partitioning** - Tables and indexes that have the potential to grow large and that are scanned frequently should be intelligently partitioned in hopes that only certain partitions, and not the entire object, will be scanned.

- **Use automatic segment management** - Tables and indexes that are the likely targets of much INSERT activity should be placed into tablespaces that use automatic segment management instead of traditional free list management (available only in Oracle9i and above). Note that LOBs cannot be stored in such tablespaces.

- **Use read only tablespaces** - Tables that will be read only should be placed into read only tablespaces.

- **Use automatic UNDO** - If Oracle9i is being used, the automatic UNDO management should be employed to alleviate the need for sizing and creating individual rollback segments

Avoiding Database Downtime

As a DBA, you do not want anything to bring down your database or cause a 'hang' that stops critical work from being done on a system. Because a storage problem has the potential to do both (especially the latter), you want to proactively put things in place that prevent any downtime.
Free space or the lack thereof, is at the heart of many storage-related problems. You should always ensure that both your server and your database have free space available when the need for more room arises. There are some very simple ways to accomplish this.

Automatic Growth

Way back in version 7, Oracle introduced the concept of auto-extendable datafiles. This simple addition to Oracle has silenced many a DBA's pager. It basically allows Oracle to automatically grow a datafile to meet the need of incoming or changed data if not enough free space currently exists in the tablespace.

To enable this feature, you can either create a tablespace with *autoextend* enabled or alter a tablespace after creation to turn the feature on. An example of creating a tablespace with *autoextend* initially enabled would be:

```
create tablespace
    users
datafile
    'd:\oracle\ora92\o92\users01.dbf' size 25600k
autoextend on next 1280k maxsize unlimited
extent management local autoallocate
logging
online;
```

Some DBAs have an aversion to using *autoextend* and instead prefer to preallocate space to a tablespace. If proper capacity planning measures are used, this approach can work just fine.

However, if the database is very dynamic and unpredictable, then *autoextend* should be enabled for most tablespaces, especially temporary tablespaces that can be the object of large sort operations.

Some DBAs may not know whether *autoextend* is enabled for their tablespaces and datafiles. Furthermore, they may not know how much total space their storage structures are currently taking up. Depending on the Oracle version you are using, one of the two following scripts can give you these exact facts.

For DBAs using Oracle7 – Oracle 8.0, the *spacesum7.sql* script can be used:

spacesum7.sql

```
select
        tablespace_name,
        decode(autoextend,null,'no','yes') autoextend,
        round ((total_space / 1024 / 1024), 2) as
        total_space,
        round ((total_free_space / 1024 / 1024), 2) as
        total_free,
        round (((total_space - total_free_space) /
        1024 / 1024), 2) as used_space,
        to_char (nvl (round ((100 * sum_free_blocks /
                    sum_alloc_blocks),2),0)) || '%'
        as pct_free
  from
        (select
                tablespace_name, max(b.inc) autoextend,
                sum (blocks) sum_alloc_blocks,
                sum (bytes) as total_space
          from
                sys.dba_data_files a,
                sys.filext$ b
          where
                b.file# (+)= a.file_id
          group by tablespace_name),
        (select
                b.tablespace_name fs_ts_name,
                nvl (sum (bytes), 0) as total_free_space,
                sum (blocks) as sum_free_blocks
          from
                dba_free_space a,
                dba_tablespaces b
          where
          a.tablespace_name (+) = b.tablespace_name
          group by b.tablespace_name,   status)
  where
        tablespace_name = fs_ts_name
  order by 1;
```

If Oracle8i and above is being used, then the *spacesum8i.sql* script will be necessary.

spacesum8i.sql

```
select
        tablespace_name,
        autoextend,
        round ((total_space / 1024 / 1024), 2) as
        total_space,
        round ((total_free_space /
        1024 / 1024), 2) as total_free,
```

```
         round (((total_space - total_free_space) /
         1024 / 1024), 2) as used_space,
         to_char (
           nvl (
             round (
               (100 *
                  sum_free_blocks /
                  sum_alloc_blocks),2),0)) || '%'
             as pct_free
  from (select
               tablespace_name,
               max (autoextensible) autoextend,
               sum (blocks) sum_alloc_blocks,
               sum (bytes) as total_space
         from
               dba_data_files
         group by tablespace_name),
         (select
               b.tablespace_name fs_ts_name,
               nvl (sum (bytes), 0) as total_free_space,
               sum (blocks) as sum_free_blocks
         from
               dba_free_space a, dba_tablespaces b
         where
               a.tablespace_name (+) = b.tablespace_name
         group by b.tablespace_name,  status)
  where
         tablespace_name = fs_ts_name
union all
select
         d.tablespace_name, autoextend,
         round ((a.bytes / 1024 / 1024), 2),
         round ((a.bytes / 1024 / 1024) -
         (nvl (t.bytes, 0) / 1024 / 1024), 2),
         round (nvl (t.bytes, 0) / 1024 / 1024, 2),
         to_char (100 - (nvl (t.bytes /
         a.bytes * 100, 0)), '990.00')
  from
         sys.dba_tablespaces d,
         (select
               tablespace_name,
               max (autoextensible) autoextend,
               sum (bytes) bytes
         from
               dba_temp_files
         group by tablespace_name) a,
         (select
               tablespace_name, sum (bytes_cached) bytes
         from
               sys.v_$temp_extent_pool
         group by tablespace_name) t
  where
         d.tablespace_name = a.tablespace_name (+)
    and d.tablespace_name = t.tablespace_name (+)
    and d.extent_management like 'LOCAL'
    and d.contents like 'TEMPORARY'
  order by 1;
```

	TABLESPACE_NAME	AUTOEXTEND	TOTAL_SPACE	TOTAL_FREE	USED_SPACE	PCT_FREE
1	AUTOSEG	NO	5	4.94	.06	98.75%
2	DRSYS	YES	20	15.19	4.81	75.94%
3	INDX	YES	25	24.88	.13	99.5%
4	OEM_REPOSITORY	YES	35.01	3	32.01	8.57%
5	SYSTEM	YES	300	3.63	296.38	1.21%
6	TEMP	YES	556	1	555	0.18
7	TOOLS	YES	10	7.75	2.25	77.5%
8	UNDOTBS1	YES	210	208.69	1.31	99.38%
9	USERS	YES	25	15.13	9.88	60.5%
10	XDB	YES	38.13	.19	37.94	.49%

Figure 4.1 – Output displaying summary space information and autoextend properties for tablespaces

While the queries above will let you know if a tablespace has autoextend enabled, it will not tell which datafile, if the tablespace has multiple datafiles. For that, you will need the *datafileae.sql* script, which will work for all Oracle versions:

datafileae.sql

```
select
      b.file_name,
      b.tablespace_name,
      decode(c.inc,null,'no','yes') autoextend
  from
      sys.dba_data_files b,
      sys.filext$ c
 where
      c.file# (+)= b.file_id
 order by
      2, 1;
```

Avoiding Database Downtime

	FILE_NAME	TABLESPACE_NAME	AUTOEXTEND
1	D:\ORACLE\ORA92\O92\AUTOSEG.ORA	AUTOSEG	NO
2	D:\ORACLE\ORA92\O92\DRSYS01.DBF	DRSYS	YES
3	D:\ORACLE\ORA92\O92\INDX01.DBF	INDX	YES
4	D:\ORACLE\ORA92\O92\OEM_REPOSITORY.DBF	OEM_REPOSITORY	YES
5	D:\ORACLE\ORA92\O92\SYSTEM01.DBF	SYSTEM	YES
6	D:\ORACLE\ORA92\O92\TOOLS01.DBF	TOOLS	YES
7	D:\ORACLE\ORA92\O92\UNDOTBS01.DBF	UNDOTBS1	YES
8	D:\ORACLE\ORA92\O92\USERS01.DBF	USERS	YES
9	D:\ORACLE\ORA92\O92\XDB01.DBF	XDB	YES

Figure 4.2 – Information regarding what datafiles have autoextend enabled

Unlimited Object Extents

When an object in Oracle (table, index, table partition, etc.) needs to expand, Oracle is kind enough to automatically allocate another extent of space to accommodate the incoming data.

Many DBAs, however, have horror stories about how a critical database suddenly froze in its tracks because a hub table or index had reached its maximum extent limit, which is the maximum number of extents that Oracle will allow an object to possess. If that limit was reached, a DBA could increase the maximum extent limit to a higher number, providing the object had not reached the ceiling of allowable extents for the Oracle version/operating system combination being used.

But if the ceiling had indeed been reached, the DBA then had no choice but to reorganize the object into fewer extents.

Such a situation can be quite time consuming, but it can be completely avoided if you create or alter your objects to have unlimited extents, which is allowed in the most recent Oracle versions (at least back to Oracle 7.3). For example, to alter an object to have unlimited extents, you can simply issue a DDL command like the following:

```
alter table
   eradmin.patient
   storage(maxextents unlimited);
```

Unlimited extents are the rule in locally-managed tablespaces, so if you choose to use these storage structures in your database, you will not have to worry about an object reaching a maximum extent limit. Still, some DBAs have expressed concerns over whether an object having hundreds or thousands of extents will experience performance problems when full table scans or similar operations are performed against them.

While most Oracle experts agree that such I/O degradation might have been experienced in earlier Oracle versions (prior to 7.3), most feel that such is not the case any longer, especially when locally-managed tablespaces are used.

If you would like proof as to whether this is actually the case, then consider the following test performed on an Oracle 8.1.5 database. An informal benchmark of whether an object that is nestled into one extent will offer better performance over an object that spans many extents can be obtained, both for like objects in dictionary-managed tablespaces and locally-managed tablespaces. The tablespaces will be placed on non-RAID drives and will have these characteristics:

```
create tablespace
```

```
    hser_lm_data
datafile
   'e:\oracle\oradata\hser\hserdata_lm.dbf'
size 100m
autoextend on next 10m maxsize unlimited
extent management local uniform size 128k;

create tablespace
   hser_lm_indexes
datafile
   'd:\oracle\oradata\hser\hseridx_lm.dbf'
size 50m
autoextend on next 10m maxsize unlimited
extent management local uniform size 128k;

create tablespace
   hser_dm_data
datafile
   'e:\oracle\oradata\hser\hserdata_dm.dbf'
size 100m
autoextend on next 10m maxsize unlimited;

create tablespace
   hser_dm_indexes
datafile
   'd:\oracle\oradata\hser\hseridx_dm.dbf'
size 50m
autoextend on next 10m maxsize unlimited;
```

The data and index tablespaces have been placed on different drives (just as good DBAs have been taught) and have identical drive placements for both locally and dictionary-managed tablespaces.

A set of identical tables and indexes will now be created in both the locally and dictionary-managed tablespaces, as we see in the listing below.

```
--
-- table: admission
--
create table admission(
    admission_id          number(38, 0)    not null,
    patient_id            number(38, 0)    not null,
    admission_timestamp   date             not null,
    admission_discharge   date,
    insured               char(1)          not null,
    release_ok            char(1)          not null,
    patient_insurance_id  number(38, 0)    not null,
    constraint admission_pk primary key (admission_id,patient_id)
)
```

```
;

comment on table admission is 'admission represents an instance of
a patient being admitted to the hospital for medical
treatment/attention'
;
--
-- table: patient
--

create table patient(
    patient_id              number(38, 0)       not null,
    patient_first_name      varchar2(20)        not null,
    patient_middle_name     varchar2(20),
    patient_last_name       varchar2(30)        not null,
    patient_ssn             number(38, 0)       not null,
    patient_address         varchar2(50)        not null,
    patient_city            varchar2(30)        not null,
    patient_state           varchar2(2)         not null,
    patient_zip             varchar2(10)        not null,
    constraint patient_pk primary key (patient_id)
)
;


comment on table patient is 'patient represents an individual
seeking medical treatment/attention'
;
--
-- index: admission_patient_id
--

create index admission_patient_id on admission(patient_id)
;
--
-- index: admission_insured
--

create bitmap index admission_insured on admission(insured)
;
--
-- index: patient_ssn
--

create unique index patient_ssn on patient(patient_ssn)
;
--
-- index: patient_last_name
--
create index patient_last_name on patient(patient_last_name)
;
```

Nothing will differ between any of the table and index
definitions except their tablespace placement. Next, two
tables in both tablespaces will be filled with data - 500,000

rows will exist in the PATIENT table and 1,000,000 rows will be moved into the ADMISSION table.

All tables and indexes will be updated with the *compute statistics* function of the *analyze* command, and the Oracle database will be run in an optimizer mode of *cost*. Afterwards, the demographics of both sets of objects look like this:

Object	Object Type	Tablespace	Rows	Extents
ADMISSION_DM	TABLE	Dictionary	1,000,000	1
ADMISSION_LM	TABLE	Locally-Managed	1,000,000	301
ADMISSION_PK_DM	PK INDEX	Dictionary		1
ADMISSION_PK_LM	PK INDEX	Locally-Managed		175
ADMISSION_INSURED_DM	BITMAP INDEX	Dictionary		1
ADMISSION_INSURED_LM	BITMAP INDEX	Locally-Managed		3
ADMISSION_PATIENT_ID_DM	B-TREE INDEX	Dictionary		1
ADMISSION_PATIENT_ID_LM	B-TREE INDEX	Locally-Managed		140
PATIENT_DM	TABLE	Dictionary	500,000	1
PATIENT_LM	TABLE	Locally-Managed	500,000	304
PATIENT_LAST_NAME_DM	B-TREE INDEX	Dictionary		1
PATIENT_LAST_NAME_LM	B-TREE INDEX	Locally-Managed		79
PATIENT_PK_DM	B-TREE INDEX	Dictionary		1
PATIENT_PK_LM	B-TREE INDEX	Locally-Managed		66
PATIENT_SSN_DM	UNIQUE INDEX	Dictionary		1
PATIENT_SSN_LM	UNIQUE INDEX	Locally-Managed		75

Table 4.1 – Object demographics for the dictionary vs. locally-managed tablespace test

In Table 4.1, notice the large number of extents that the objects in the locally-managed tablespace consume, whereas each object in the dictionary-managed tablespaces consists of only one extent each.

Next, each set of objects will be put through identical tests. The following table lists informal benchmark results from a variety of SQL related and Oracle utility operations on both the dictionary and locally-managed tablespaces. SQL access paths have been verified as identical through EXPLAIN analysis.

Operation	Access Path/ Explanation	Rows Affected /Returned	Dictionary	Locally- Managed
			(response time in seconds)	
SELECT	Full table scan count on PATIENT	500,000	4	5
SELECT	Full table scan count on ADMISSION	1,000,000	5	5
SELECT	Merge join between PATIENT and ADMISSION (full table scan on PATIENT, non-unique index scan on ADMISSION)	1	111	111
SELECT	Unique index access on PATIENT (PATIENT_SSN)	1	.25	.25
SELECT	Non-Unique index access on PATIENT (PATIENT_LAST_NAME)	2	1	1
SELECT	Unique index access on ADMISSION	1	.25	.25
SELECT	Non-Unique index access on ADMISSION (PATIENT_ID)	2	.30	.30
SELECT	Bitmap index access on ADMISSION	1	.5	.5
SELECT CURSOR	Loop through every record in PATIENT with cursor reading PATIENT_ID into declared	500,000	38	39

Operation	Access Path/ Explanation	Rows Affected /Returned	Dictionary	Locally- Managed
			(response time in seconds)	
	variable. Sort (ASC) performed on PATIENT_ID			
UPDATE	Full UPDATE on RELEASE_OK column of ADMISSION	1,000,000	350	355
DELETE	Full DELETE from PATIENT (no COMMIT's)	500,000	872	841
EXPORT	FULL PATIENT TABLE (conventional)	500,000	36	35
IMPORT	FULL PATIENT TABLE (conventional, structure and indexes already in place)	500,000	349	340
ANALYZE	COMPUTE STATISTICS on ADMISSION TABLE	1,000,000	326	326
TOTALS			2,093.3	2,059.3

Table 4.2 – Benchmark results for the dictionary vs. locally-managed tablespace test

Table 4.2 shows the locally-managed tablespaces squeezing out a 34 second victory over the dictionary-managed tablespaces, primarily due to the margins obtained in the full DELETE and IMPORT operations. Clearly, at least for this informal testing procedure, overall performance does not suffer one bit for objects that comprise hundreds of extents in a locally-managed tablespace vs. objects contained in a single extent in a dictionary-managed tablespace.

The last thing to keep in mind regarding objects with unlimited extents is that it is still possible for an object not to be able to extend, even if it has an unlimited extent limit. The three primary reasons an object will fail to extend include:

- **No file autoextend** - The tablespace that the object resides in does not have autoextend enabled, and there is not enough room in the tablespace to add the object's new extent

- **No filesystem space** - The tablespace that the object resides in has autoextend enabled, but the drive/file system that the tablespace is on is out of free space and will not allow the tablespace to automatically grow.

- **Fragmentation problem** - The dictionary managed tablespace that the object resides in has enough total free space to add the object's new extent, but the free space is not contiguous in nature (because of bubble fragmentation), and therefore, the object cannot extend.

Bubble fragmentation, as well as general fragmentation, will be covered further in an upcoming section.

Preventing Transactional Failures

Nothing makes a DBA's heart sink further than a situation where a monster transaction fails because of space reasons. Many times, not only does the transaction fail, but immediately afterwards a giant system rollback begins that can take longer to complete than the transaction itself.

If you are using Oracle9i, you can reduce such situations to only a bad memory. The 9i resumable space allocation feature provides a method where a transaction is actually suspended when one of these storage related problems occurs:

- An out-of-space condition takes places (tablespace runs out of free space, etc.)
- An object reaches its maximum extent limit
- A space quota is exceeded

This feature allows a DBA to enter the picture and correct the space problem. Once fixed, the transaction actually resumes and nothing is lost.

There are a number of hoops you must jump through to enable resumable space allocation, so if this feature appeals to you, you should consult the Oracle9i documentation (Administrators guide) for the full story on how to make it work.

Operating System Checks

As a DBA you need to be aware of the space situation not only in your database, but also at the server level. Having tablespaces that can automatically grow and objects that can always extend will not help you much, if the actual server hasn't enough space to answer Oracle's demands.

You should always keep an eye on the free space reserves that exist in the following database server locations:

- The drives/file systems that hold tablespace data files

- The drives/file systems that serve as the destination for archive log files

- The drives/file systems that hold database backups and export dumps

All these areas on your database server should have ample room to meet the database's current and future needs.

Critical Storage Headaches to Avoid

As much as possible, you want to be proactive in your approach to Oracle storage management. Naturally, the first step in this is ensuring that you have intelligently planned for the current and future space needs of your database (both inside the database and outside on the server), and are using all the ammunition that Oracle provides you with respect to space-related features.

While this is all well and good for new databases, you might inherit an existing database that is not in tiptop shape from a storage standpoint. What sort of investigating should you do on such databases to determine their storage health, and how should you work to keep any new databases free from space-related headaches?

Fragmentation Issues

Handling space fragmentation in Oracle used to be a major pain for DBAs. But as we have already discussed, recent advances in the Oracle database engine have made life much easier for administrators to manage space and prevent storage-related outages.

The advents of auto-growth datafiles, locally-managed tablespaces, and built-in reorganization abilities have caused many a DBA's pager to go silent. Even so, fragmentation is still an issue that a DBA must deal with from time to time. What types of fragmentation should a DBA be on the lookout for, and when does it truly represent a problem that needs attention?

First, you need to understand the different types of fragmentation that can occur in your database, and then you can go about rectifying the situation should a fragmentation problem be found.

Fragmentation Types

There are two broad categories of fragmentation that a DBA will encounter: tablespace and object fragmentation. With respect to tablespace fragmentation, administrators have traditionally fought two types: free space honeycombs and free space bubbles. Honeycomb fragmentation is really not difficult to detect or handle.

Tablespace Fragmentation

Basically, honeycomb fragmentation occurs when two free space extents in a tablespace reside beside each other. For example, rather than having one large free space extent of 5MB, a tablespace might have two extents that are next to each other (a honeycomb) that make up 2MB and 3MB. If an incoming object required a single 4MB extent allocation, Oracle would have to coalesce the honeycomb to make room for the object.

The necessary coalesce operation would cause a small degree of performance degradation. However, the situation would be resolved and no space-related bottleneck would remain. Fragmentation bubbles, however, are another story and are the traditional reason DBAs have had to perform full tablespace reorganizations.

Bubbles occur when objects are continuously added and dropped in a tablespace, with the end result being free space pockets (or bubbles) being interspersed between objects that remain in the tablespace. This can become problematic when, for example, an incoming object requires a single 5MB extent allocation, but there is not enough contiguous space in the tablespace to meet the demand.

Even if the total amount of free space in the tablespace equals the required 5MB, it will do no good if that 5MB is made up of 5 non-contiguous blocks of free space. In this situation, Oracle has no alternative but to either extend the datafile to make room for the object (if the tablespace's datafile has the AUTOEXTEND property enabled), or return an error and deny the object entry into the tablespace.

Object Fragmentation

Object fragmentation headaches generally take one of two forms. The first is extent fragmentation, where the object in question has extended into so many space extents that it is nearing its maximum extent limit, a topic discussed in the prior section.

A true bottleneck risk is indeed present in dictionary-managed tablespaces when an object nears its maximum extent limit. If the limit is reached, then Oracle returns an error and data additions to the object will be denied until space is either freed up within the object, the object is reorganized, or the DBA increases the object's maximum extent limit.

The second form of object fragmentation revolves around what is called a table's "high water mark". Tables that are the victim of much insert-delete activity can develop performance problems due to wasted space being present. A table's high-water mark equals the last block in the table that was used to hold data. The problem in Oracle is that this high-water mark is not reset by DELETE activity, so it is possible for a table to have absolutely no data in it but contain a high-water mark that is many blocks high.

When such a table is scanned, Oracle will read up to the high-water mark even if no rows exist in the table at all. This can make for some unnecessarily large scan times (see the first section in this chapter for a real world example). Like tables, indexes with large amounts of insert-delete activity can end up having extended B-tree depths and many deleted (wasted) leaf row blocks.

Detecting Tablespace Fragmentation

How can you tell if your tablespaces are suffering from fragmentation problems and then identify the type of fragmentation? The detection and diagnosis is not hard to make at all. To determine if your tablespaces are having a problem with fragmentation, you can use the *tsfrag.sql* script:

---

tsfrag.sql

```
select
        tablespace_name,
        count(*) free_chunks,
        decode(round((max(bytes) / 1024000),2),null,0,
        round((max(bytes) / 1024000),2)) largest_chunk,
        nvl(round(sqrt(max(blocks)/sum(blocks))*
        (100/sqrt(sqrt(count(blocks)) )),2),0)
        fragmentation_index
from
        sys.dba_free_space
group by
        tablespace_name
order by
        2 desc, 1;
```

	TABLESPACE_NAME	FREE_CHUNKS	LARGEST_CHUNK	FRAGMENTATION_INDEX
1	TEMP	2208	.44	.81
2	USER_DATA	73	63.23	31.33
3	RBS	36	18.94	15.77
4	USER_DATA2	8	4.66	57.06
5	ER_DATA	5	2.47	47.33
6	BROKER_DATA	3	8.26	72.94
7	BROKER_INDEXES	1	10.18	100
8	OEM_REPOSITORY	1	2.82	100
9	USER_DATA3	1	12.28	100
10	SYSTEM	1	.24	100
11	TEST	1	1.02	100
12	TEST_TS	1	14.27	100
13	TOOLS	1	5.08	100
14	USER_INDEXES	1	.38	100

Figure 4.3 - Checking for tablespace fragmentation

When you examine the script output, you need to hone in on a couple of columns in particular. First, notice the fragmentation index column. This will give your tablespace an overall ranking with respect to how badly it is actually

---

fragmented. A 100% score indicates no fragmentation at all. Lesser scores verify the presence of fragmentation.

The free chunks count column will tell you how many segments of free space are scattered throughout the tablespace. One thing to keep in mind is that tablespaces with multiple datafiles will always show a free chunk count greater than one because each datafile will likely have at least one pocket of free space.

If you want to drill down a little further and find out how badly fragmented each datafile in your database is, you can use the *dffrag.sql* script:

dffrag.sql

```
select
      b.file_name, b.tablespace_name,
      nvl(round(sqrt(max(a.blocks)/
      sum(a.blocks))*(100/sqrt(sqrt(count(a.blocks)) )),2),0)
      fragmentation_index,
      decode(c.inc,null,'no','yes') autoextend,
      count (*) free_chunks,
      decode (
          round ((max (a.bytes) / 1024000), 2),
          null, 0,
          round ((max (a.bytes) / 1024000), 2)) largest_chunk
  from
        sys.dba_free_space a,
        sys.dba_data_files b,
        sys.filext$ c
 where
        b.tablespace_name = a.tablespace_name (+) and
        c.file# (+)= a.file_id and
        b.file_id = a.file_id (+)
 group
        by b.file_name,
        decode(c.inc,null,'no','yes'),
        b.tablespace_name
 order
        by 5 desc, 1;
```

	FILE_NAME	TABLESPACE_NAME	FRAGMENTATION_INDEX	AUTOEXTEND	FREE_CHUNKS	LARGEST_CHUNK
1	D:\ORACLE\ORADATA\O817\TEMP01.DBF	TEMP	.81	YES	2208	.44
2	D:\ORACLE\ORADATA\O817\USERS01.DBF	USER_DATA	32.08	YES	68	63.23
3	D:\ORACLE\ORADATA\O817\RBS01.DBF	RBS	15.77	YES	36	18.94
4	D:\ORACLE\ORADATA\O817\USER_DATA2.DBF	USER_DATA2	57.06	NO	8	4.66
5	D:\ORACLE\ORADATA\O817\ER_DATA.DBF	ER_DATA	47.33	NO	5	2.47
6	D:\ORACLE\ORADATA\O817\USERS02.DBF	USER_DATA	43.98	YES	5	.38
7	D:\ORACLE\ORADATA\O817\BROKER_DATA.DBF	BROKER_DATA	72.94	YES	3	8.26
8	D:\ORACLE\ORADATA\O817\BIGADMIN.DBF	BIG_ADMISSION	0	NO	1	0
9	D:\ORACLE\ORADATA\O817\BROKER_INDEXES.DBF	BROKER_INDEXES	100	YES	1	10.18
10	D:\ORACLE\ORADATA\O817\INDX01.DBF	USER_INDEXES	100	YES	1	.38
11	D:\ORACLE\ORADATA\O817\OEM_REPOSITORY.ORA	OEM_REPOSITORY	100	YES	1	2.82
12	D:\ORACLE\ORADATA\O817\USER_DATA3.DBF	USER_DATA3	100	NO	1	12.28
13	D:\ORACLE\ORADATA\O817\SYSTEM01.DBF	SYSTEM	100	YES	1	.24
14	D:\ORACLE\ORADATA\O817\TEST01.DBF	TEST	100	YES	1	1.02
15	D:\ORACLE\ORADATA\O817\TEST_TS.ORA	TEST_TS	100	YES	1	14.27
16	D:\ORACLE\ORADATA\O817\TOOLS01.DBF	TOOLS	100	YES	1	5.08

Figure 4.4 - Checking for datafile fragmentation

One last thing to remember in detecting tablespace fragmentation is that even if you find numerous free chunk counts in locally-managed tablespaces, it really is not an issue.

Since every object placed in the tablespace will have the same extent size, sooner or later the pockets of free space will be reused, whether new objects are placed into the tablespace or existing objects extend.

If you indeed find fragmentation in your tablespaces, you should identify whether it is of the honeycomb or bubble variety.

To answer this question, you need to produce a tablespace 'map' that plots the entire tablespace in datafile/block id order. Doing so will show you a number of interesting things, including where the actual objects in the tablespace reside, along with where the pockets of free space are located.

A clean tablespace will normally show one large segment of free space at the end. A badly fragmented tablespace will show bubbles of free space interspersed throughout. Two

Critical Storage Headaches to Avoid

free space segments that reside next to one another can identify honeycombs.

A good tablespace map script for version 7 of Oracle is the *tsmap7.sql*:

---

tsmap7.sql

```
select
        'free space' object_owner,
        '    ' object_type,
        '    ' object_name,
        file_id,
        block_id,
        bytes / 1024 size_kb,
        blocks
from
        sys.dba_free_space
where
        tablespace_name = <:tablespace name>
union all
select
        owner,
        segment_type,
        segment_name,
        file_id,
        block_id,
        bytes / 1024,
        blocks
from
        sys.dba_extents
where
        tablespace_name = <:tablespace name>
order by
        4,5;
```

If version 8 or higher of Oracle is being used, then the *tsmap8.sql* script should be used:

---

tsmap8.sql

```
select
        'free space' object_owner,
        '    ' object_type,
        '    ' object_name,
        file_id,
        block_id,
```

```
        bytes / 1024 size_kb,
        blocks
from
        sys.dba_free_space
where
        tablespace_name = <:tablespace name>
union all
select
        owner,
        segment_type,
        decode (partition_name,null,segment_name,segment_name ||
        '.' || partition_name),
        file_id,
        block_id,
        bytes / 1024,
        blocks
from
        sys.dba_extents
where
        tablespace_name = <:tablespace name>
order by
        4,5;
```

	OBJECT_OWNER	OBJECT_TYPE	OBJECT_NAME	FILE_ID	BLOCK_ID	SIZE_KB	BLOCKS
1	USER21	TABLE	TAB1	3	2	128	16
2	ERADMIN	INDEX	PK22	3	18	128	16
3	free space			3	34	128	16
4	USER21	TABLE	INDEX1	3	50	128	16
5	EMBT_CP	INDEX	REF61	3	66	128	16
6	EMBT_CP	INDEX	REF63	3	82	128	16
7	EMBT_CP	INDEX	REF62	3	98	128	16
8	free space			3	114	128	16
9	ERADMIN	LOBSEGMENT	SYS_LOB0000034196C00001$$	3	130	128	16
10	free space			3	146	128	16
11	EMBT_CP	TABLE	CP_TABLE	3	162	128	16
12	EMBT_CP	INDEX	REF67	3	178	128	16
13	ERADMIN	TABLE	TEST_RAW	3	194	128	16
14	BILLY	TABLE	PLAN_TABLE	3	210	128	16
15	ERADMIN	TABLE	EMP_BKP	3	226	128	16
16	ERADMIN	TABLE	CREATE$JAVA$LOB$TABLE	3	242	128	16
17	BAD_GUY	TABLE	ROB	3	258	128	16
18	ERADMIN	TABLE	DOCTOR_PROCEDURE	3	274	128	16
19	ERADMIN	INDEX	PK10	3	290	128	16
20	ERADMIN	TABLE	EMPLOYEE	3	306	128	16
21	ERADMIN	TABLE	MEDICATION	3	322	128	16
22	ERADMIN	INDEX	PK11	3	338	128	16
23	ERADMIN	TABLE	MEDICATION_DISP	3	354	128	16
24	ERADMIN	INDEX	PK12	3	370	128	16
25	ERADMIN	TABLE	MEDICATION_DISPM	3	386	128	16
26	ERADMIN	INDEX	PK13	3	402	128	16
27	ERADMIN	TABLE	NURSE	3	418	128	16
28	ERADMIN	LOBINDEX	SYS_IL0000034192C00002$$	3	434	128	16

Figure 4.5 - Mapping the contents of a tablespace

Eliminating Tablespace Fragmentation

Once you identify tablespace fragmentation, what do you do about it? Honeycomb fragmentation is easy to fix. All that needs to be done is to combine adjacent free segments into one by issuing a coalesce statement similar to this:

```
alter tablespace USERS coalesce;
```

Bubble fragmentation is more difficult to handle. Of course, the best course of action is to prevent it in the first place. And as discussed earlier, the best weapon for this is to use locally-managed tablespaces. It may sound too simple, but in reality, implementing these storage structures in your database can just about remove the need to perform full tablespace reorganizations.

However, what do you do if you are in a situation where you have many databases that were set up with dictionary-managed tablespaces? You have two options, at least if you are running Oracle 8i (the version that gave birth to locally-managed tablespaces). First, you can create new locally-managed tablespaces in your database and then perform one last, full tablespace reorganization of all the database objects into the new tablespaces.

Needless to say, this can be a difficult task if you have large databases and no third-party reorganization tool. However, it will be worth the effort as you will likely never have to reorganize your tablespaces again, *and* your objects should never again encounter a maximum extent limit.

If you are using Oracle 8.1.6 or higher, you can convert any current dictionary-managed tablespaces to locally-managed tablespaces. Buried in the Oracle documentation is a procedure for converting a tablespace's extent management from dictionary to local or vice-versa.

The additions to the *sys.dbms_space_admin* package make it quite simple to convert a tablespace to locally-managed (or to convert a locally-managed tablespace to dictionary-managed if desired). For example, if you want to convert a dictionary-managed tablespace, called USERS to locally-managed in Oracle; all you would have to do is issue this single command:

```
sys.dbms_space_admin.tablespace_migrate_to_local('USERS')
```

If you are afraid of how long this procedure might take on large tablespaces, do not be. It actually runs very fast. If, for some reason, you would like to take a tablespace that is locally-managed back to dictionary management, you can issue this command:

```
sys.dbms_space_admin.tablespace_migrate_from_local('USERS')
```

There are a few restrictions on these conversion procedures (for example, 9i UNDO tablespaces currently cannot be converted, etc.), so you should check the Oracle documentation for the specifics of using these new procedures. Also, note that converting a dictionary-managed tablespace that has existing objects to local will not magically rebuild all the existing object extents to conform to the sizing guidelines used by locally-managed tablespaces.

If your situation precludes the use of locally-managed tablespaces, what choices are you left with to control tablespace fragmentation? One thing you can do is

---

manually mimicking the mechanisms of locally-managed tablespaces. This is done by:

- Creating a tablespace that has same-sized extents for every object's INITIAL and NEXT extent values

- Setting the tablespace's PCTINCREASE property to zero

- Creating new objects in the tablespace *without* storage properties so they will inherit the tablespace's default storage properties

- Setting each object's maximum extent limit to unlimited

Detecting Object Fragmentation

Object fragmentation can damage your performance in one of two ways:

- If you have objects in dictionary-managed tablespaces that have a maximum extent limit set to something other than unlimited, then your objects could run out of space

- As a result of repeated insert and delete activity, tables can become internally fragmented and contain a lot of wasted space. In the same way, indexes can become fragmented so that their depth reaches unacceptable levels. This predicament will be covered in the next section.

How can you tell if your objects are getting close to hitting their maximum extent limit? This is quite easy to do. If you are using version 7 of Oracle, then you can execute the *maxext7.sql* script, which will find all objects that are within five extents of their limit:

---

maxext7.sql

```
select
        owner,
        segment_name,
        segment_type,
        extents,
        max_extents,
        initial_extent,
        next_extent,
        tablespace_name
from
        sys.dba_segments
where
        max_extents - extents <= 5 and
        segment_type <> 'CACHE'
order by
        1,2,3;
```

If you are using version 8 or higher of Oracle, then you can use the *maxext8.sql* script:

---

maxext8.sql

```
select
        owner,
        decode(partition_name,NULL,segment_name,segment_name ||
        '.' || partition_name) segment_name,
        segment_type,
        extents,
        max_extents,
        initial_extent,
        next_extent,
        tablespace_name
from
        sys.dba_segments
where
        max_extents - extents <= 5 and
        segment_type <> 'CACHE'
order by
        1,2,3;
```

	OWNER	SEGMENT_NAME	SEGMENT_TYPE	EXTENTS	MAX_EXTENTS	INITIAL_EXTENT	NEXT_EXTENT	TABLESPACE_NAME
1	ERADMIN	CANT_EXTEND	TABLE	3	4	131072	131072	USER_DATA
2	USER21	TABLE1	TABLE	1	1	16384	6144000	USER_DATA
3	USER21	TABLE2	TABLE	1	1	106496	8192	USER_DATA
4	USER21	TABLE3	TABLE	1	1	106496	8192	USER_DATA

Figure 4.6 - Output showing objects nearing their maximum extent limit

Another extent problem arises when an object in a dictionary-managed tablespace cannot extend because of a lack of contiguous free space. To uncover these types of problems, you can use the *objdef.sql* script:

objdef.sql

```
select
    a.owner,
    a.segment_name,
    a.segment_type,
    a.tablespace_name,
    a.next_extent,
    max(c.bytes) max_contig_space
from
    sys.dba_segments a,
    sys.dba_free_space c
where
    a.tablespace_name = c.tablespace_name and
    a.next_extent >
      (select
            max(bytes)
       from
            sys.dba_free_space b
       where
            a.tablespace_name = b.tablespace_name and
            b.tablespace_name = c.tablespace_name)
group by
        a.owner,
        a.segment_name,
        a.tablespace_name,
        a.segment_type,
        a.next_extent
```

	OWNER	SEGMENT_NAME	SEGMENT_TYPE	TABLESPACE_NAME	NEXT_EXTENT	MAX_CONTIG_SPACE
1	BAD_GUY	ADMISSION	TABLE PARTITION	USER_DATA	104857600	64749568
2	ERADMIN	ADMISSION	TABLE PARTITION	USER_DATA	104857600	64749568
3	ERADMIN	REF440	INDEX	USER_DATA	102400000	64749568
4	USER21	TABLE1	TABLE	USER_DATA	6144000	4767744
5	SYS	C_FILE#_BLOCK#	CLUSTER	SYSTEM	335872	245760
6	SYS	EMBARCADERO_EXPLAIN_PLAN	TABLE	SYSTEM	507904	245760
7	SYS	I_IDL_SB41	INDEX	SYSTEM	335872	245760
8	SYS	I_IDL_UB11	INDEX	SYSTEM	1146880	245760
9	SYS	I_IDL_UB21	INDEX	SYSTEM	335872	245760
10	SYS	JAVANM	TABLE	SYSTEM	507904	245760

Figure 4.7 - Output showing objects that have a space deficit in their parent tablespace

Correcting Object Fragmentation

The prescription for correcting object fragmentation is generally total object reorganization. Such a procedure used to be fraught with errors and fear, even when third party software products were used. Fortunately, this is not really the case any longer, as Oracle has provided more built-in reorganization capabilities with each new release. Oracle has even gone so far as to grant online reorganization abilities for certain object types.

The next section will cover in detail the reorganization techniques and methods you can use to fix your objects when you discover they need to be reorganized.

Removing Storage-related Performance Vampires

While storage-related problems can cause an instant 'hang' in an otherwise well-running database, they can also slowly rob a system of its good performance over time. This happens when once well-organized objects become, well, *not* so well-organized. Such things can be hard to diagnose, but not when you know what to look for.

Detecting Space-related Object Performance Problems

What are some of the space-related object problems that you should be on the lookout for? With respect to tables, there are at least two different anomalies that can cause you problems.

Table Diagnostics

The problem of wasted space in a table and a corresponding misleading high water mark has already been discussed in this chapter. Needless to say, tables that suffer from high levels of wasted space could definitely be causing your database to spin in ways you do not want. The other problem that might exist in your tables is one of chained/migrated rows.

Under normal circumstances, a row of data should fit completely inside one Oracle block. Sometimes, however, this is not the case, and the table suddenly finds itself containing chained or migrated rows, which are rows that span more than one data block.

Chaining occurs when a row is initially too large to fit inside one block. Two or more blocks are used by Oracle to hold the row. Migration deals with rows that have grown so much that they can no longer be contained within their original block. When this occurs, Oracle relocates the row out of its original block into another block, but leaves a pointer behind to indicate the relocation.

Both chaining and migration force Oracle to perform more than one I/O to retrieve data that could normally be obtained with a single I/O operation. The end result is degraded performance.

How can you determine the levels of wasted space in your tables, plus find out if they suffer from a chained/migrated row problem? The scripts below will provide all the answers you should need. They locate tables that contain 25% or more wasted space.

As a bonus, the scripts also calculate the chained row ratio for a table, the percentage of used extents to maximum extents, and determine if the object can extend into its next block of free space.

In other words, these are nice reorganization diagnostic scripts. If you are using version 7 of Oracle, you can use the *tabreorg7.sql* script:

tabreorg7.sql

```
select
          owner,
          segment_name table_name,
          segment_type,
          round(bytes/1024,2) table_kb,
          num_rows,
          blocks,
          empty_blocks,
          hwm highwater_mark,
          avg_used_blocks,
          greatest(round(100 * (nvl(hwm - avg_used_blocks,0) /
          greatest(nvl(hwm,1),1) ),2),0) block_inefficiency,
          chain_pct,
          max_extent_pct,
          extents,
          max_extents,
          decode(greatest(max_free_space -
          next_extent,0),0,'n','y') can_extend_space,
          next_extent,
          max_free_space,
          o_tablespace_name tablespace_name
from
(select
          a.owner owner,
          segment_name,
```

```
        segment_type,
        bytes,
        num_rows,
        a.blocks blocks,
        b.empty_blocks empty_blocks,
        a.blocks - b.empty_blocks - 1 hwm,
        decode(round((b.avg_row_len * num_rows *
        (1 + (pct_free/100))) /
        c.blocksize,0),0,1,round((b.avg_row_len * num_rows *
        (1 + (pct_free/100))) / c.blocksize,0)) + 2
        avg_used_blocks,
        round(100 * (nvl(b.chain_cnt,0) /
        greatest(nvl(b.num_rows,1),1)),2)
        chain_pct,
        a.extents extents,
        round(100 * (a.extents / a.max_extents),2) max_extent_pct,
        a.max_extents max_extents,
        b.next_extent next_extent,
        b.tablespace_name o_tablespace_name
    from
        sys.dba_segments a,
        sys.dba_tables b,
        sys.ts$ c
    where
        ( a.owner = b.owner ) and
        ( segment_name = table_name ) and
        ( ( segment_type = 'table' ) ) and
        b.tablespace_name = c.name),
(   select
        tablespace_name f_tablespace_name,
        max(bytes) max_free_space
    from
        sys.dba_free_space
    group by
        tablespace_name)
    where
        f_tablespace_name = o_tablespace_name and
        greatest(round(100 * (nvl(hwm - avg_used_blocks,0) /
        greatest(nvl(hwm,1),1) ),2),0) > 25
order by
      10 desc, 1 asc,2 desc;
```

If you using Oracle8 or higher, then use the *tabreorg8.sql* script:

---

tabreorg8.sql

```
select
        /*+ RULE */
        owner,
        segment_name table_name,
        segment_type,
        round(bytes/1024,2) table_kb,
        num_rows,
```

```
        blocks,
        empty_blocks,
        hwm highwater_mark,
        avg_used_blocks,
        greatest(round(100 * (nvl(hwm - avg_used_blocks,0) /
        greatest(nvl(hwm,1),1) ),2),0) block_inefficiency,
        chain_pct,
        max_extent_pct,
        extents,
        max_extents,
        decode(greatest(max_free_space -
        next_extent,0),0,'n','y') can_extend_space,
        next_extent,
        max_free_space,
        o_tablespace_name tablespace_name
from
(select
        a.owner owner,
        segment_name,
        segment_type,
        bytes,
        num_rows,
        a.blocks blocks,
        b.empty_blocks empty_blocks,
        a.blocks - b.empty_blocks - 1 hwm,
        decode(round((b.avg_row_len * num_rows *
        (1 + (pct_free/100))) /
        c.blocksize,0),0,1,round((b.avg_row_len * num_rows *
        (1 + (pct_free/100))) / c.blocksize,0)) + 2
        avg_used_blocks,
        round(100 * (nvl(b.chain_cnt,0) /
        greatest(nvl(b.num_rows,1),1)),2)
        chain_pct,
        a.extents extents,
        round(100 * (a.extents / a.max_extents),2) max_extent_pct,
        a.max_extents max_extents,
        b.next_extent next_extent,
        b.tablespace_name o_tablespace_name
    from
        sys.dba_segments a,
        sys.dba_all_tables b,
        sys.ts$ c
  where
        ( a.owner = b.owner ) and
        ( segment_name = table_name ) and
        ( ( segment_type = 'TABLE ) ) and
        b.tablespace_name = c.name
  union all
  select
        a.owner owner,
        segment_name || '.' || b.partition_name,
        segment_type,
        bytes,
        b.num_rows,
        a.blocks blocks,
        b.empty_blocks empty_blocks,
        a.blocks - b.empty_blocks - 1 hwm,
        decode(round((b.avg_row_len * b.num_rows * (1 +
        (b.pct_free/100))) /
```

```
        c.blocksize,0),0,1,round((b.avg_row_len * b.num_rows *
        (1 + (b.pct_free/100))) / c.blocksize,0)) + 2
        avg_used_blocks,
        round(100 * (nvl(b.chain_cnt,0) /
        greatest(nvl(b.num_rows,1),1)),2)
        chain_pct,
        a.extents extents,
        round(100 * (a.extents / a.max_extents),2) max_extent_pct,
        a.max_extents max_extents,
        b.next_extent,
        b.tablespace_name o_tablespace_name
   from
        sys.dba_segments a,
        sys.dba_tab_partitions b,
        sys.ts$ c,
        sys.dba_tables d
   where
        ( a.owner = b.table_owner ) and
        ( segment_name = b.table_name ) and
        ( ( segment_type = TABLE PARTITION' ) ) and
        b.tablespace_name = c.name and
        d.owner = b.table_owner and
        d.table_name = b.table_name and
        a.partition_name = b.partition_name),
( select
        tablespace_name f_tablespace_name,
        max(bytes) max_free_space
   from
        sys.dba_free_space
   group by tablespace_name)
   where
        f_tablespace_name = o_tablespace_name and
        greatest(round(100 * (nvl(hwm - avg_used_blocks,0) /
        greatest(nvl(hwm,1),1) ),2),0) > 25
order by 10 desc, 1 asc,2 asc
```

	OWNER	TABLE_NAME	SEGMENT_TYPE	TABLE_KB	NUM_ROWS	BLOCKS	EMPTY_BLOCKS	HIGHWATER_MARK	AVG_USED_BLOCKS	BLOCK_INEFFICIENCY	CHAIN_PCT
1	ERADMIN	EMP	TABLE	19072	0	2384	120	2263	3	99.87	0
2	SYS	OBJ$	TABLE	2440	4387	305	1	303	43	85.81	0
3	SYS	ADMISSION_NO	TABLE	256	1520	32	0	31	5	83.87	0
4	USER21	TABLE1	TABLE	256	0	32	15	16	3	81.25	0
5	USER21	TABLE2	TABLE	256	130	32	12	19	4	78.95	0
6	USER21	TABLE3	TABLE	176	40	22	0	21	11	47.62	82.5
7	ERADMIN	EMBARCADERO	TABLE	384	2217	48	6	41	27	34.15	0
8	SYS	PROCEDURE$	TABLE	80	418	10	3	6	4	33.33	0
9	BRKADMIN	INVESTMENT	TABLE	64	412	8	0	7	5	28.57	0

Figure 4.8 – Partial output showing the wasted space amounts and chained row percentage of database tables.

If you want to see the shape that all your database tables are in, then you can remove the *where* clause that restricts the output to only those tables having a block efficiency ranking of 25% or higher.

There are a couple of columns in Figure 3.8 that you should hone in on. The block inefficiency ranking will highlight any table that suffers from a lot of wasted space. For example, the ERADMIN.EMP table has no rows in it but sports a very high water mark.

Therefore, it tops the list in terms of tables with high amounts of wasted space. Also, notice the chain percent column. This column indicates how badly the table suffers from chained or migrated rows. In Figure 3.8, the USER21.TABLE3 table appears to be in bad shape with respect to chained/migrated rows. Generally, if a table appears to have a chain percent of 25% or more, then you should look into reorganizing it.

Index Diagnostics

Like tables, indexes can become disorganized due to heavy DML activity. There has been much debate in the DBA world as to what you should look for when determining if an index is in poor shape, but the script below should help.

The script displays the level and clustering factor of the index, calculates the percentage of used extents to maximum extents, and also determines if the index can extend into its next block of free space. For version 7 of Oracle, use the *idxreorg7.sql* script:

---

idxreorg7.sql

```
select
        owner,
        segment_name index_name,
        segment_type,
        round(bytes/1024,2) index_kb,
        clustering_factor,
```

```
        blevel,
        blocks,
        max_extent_pct,
        extents,
        max_extents,
        decode(greatest(max_free_space -
        next_extent,0),0,'n','y') can_extend_space,
        next_extent,
        max_free_space,
        o_tablespace_name
from
(select
        a.owner owner,
        segment_name,
        segment_type,
        bytes,
        b.clustering_factor,
        b.blevel,
        a.blocks blocks,
        a.extents extents,
        round(100 * (a.extents / a.max_extents),2)
        max_extent_pct,
        a.max_extents max_extents,
        b.next_extent next_extent,
        b.tablespace_name o_tablespace_name
    from
        sys.dba_segments a,
        sys.dba_indexes b,
        sys.ts$ c
    where
        ( a.owner = b.owner ) and
        ( segment_name = index_name ) and
        ( ( segment_type = 'INDEX' ) ) and
        b.tablespace_name = c.name),
(   select
    tablespace_name f_tablespace_name,
    max(bytes) max_free_space
    from
    sys.dba_free_space
    group by tablespace_name)
where
    f_tablespace_name = o_tablespace_name
order
    by 1,2;
```

For Oracle8 and higher, use the *idxreorg8.sql* script:

---

idxreorg8.sql

```
select
        /*+ RULE */
        owner,
        segment_name index_name,
        segment_type,
        round(bytes/1024,2) index_kb,
```

```
                num_rows,
                clustering_factor,
                blevel,
                blocks,
                max_extent_pct,
                extents,
                max_extents,
                decode(greatest(max_free_space -
                next_extent,0),0,'n','y') can_extend_space,
                next_extent,
                max_free_space,
                o_tablespace_name
        from
        (select
                a.owner owner,
                segment_name,
                segment_type,
                bytes,
                num_rows,
                b.clustering_factor,
                b.blevel,
                a.blocks blocks,
                a.extents extents,
                round(100 * (a.extents / a.max_extents),2)
                max_extent_pct,
                a.max_extents max_extents,
                b.next_extent next_extent,
                b.tablespace_name o_tablespace_name
            from
                sys.dba_segments a,
                sys.dba_indexes b,
                sys.ts$ c
           where
                ( a.owner = b.owner ) and
                ( segment_name = index_name ) and
                ( ( segment_type = 'INDEX' ) ) and
                b.tablespace_name = c.name
        union all
        select
                a.owner owner,
                segment_name || '.' || b.partition_name,
                segment_type,
                bytes,
                b.num_rows,
                b.clustering_factor,
                b.blevel,
                a.blocks blocks,
                a.extents extents,
                round(100 * (a.extents / a.max_extents),2)
                max_extent_pct,
                a.max_extents max_extents,
                b.next_extent,
                b.tablespace_name o_tablespace_name
            from
                sys.dba_segments a,
                sys.dba_ind_partitions b,
                sys.ts$ c,
                sys.dba_indexes d
           where
```

```
        ( a.owner = b.index_owner ) and
        ( segment_name = b.index_name ) and
        ( ( segment_type = INDEX_PARTITION' ) ) and
        b.tablespace_name = c.name and
        d.owner = b.index_owner and
        d.index_name = b.index_name and
        a.partition_name = b.partition_name),
( select
        tablespace_name f_tablespace_name,
        max(bytes) max_free_space
    from
        sys.dba_free_space
    group by tablespace_name)
where
    f_tablespace_name = o_tablespace_name
order
    by 1,2;
```

	OWNER	INDEX_NAME	SEGMENT_TYPE	INDEX_KB	NUM_ROWS	CLUSTERING_FACTOR	BLEVEL	BLOCKS	MAX_EXTENT_PCT	EXT
7	AURORAJISUTILTY$	SNS$NODE_INDEX	INDEX	64	84	10	0	8	0	
8	AURORAJISUTILTY$	SNS$PERM_INDEX	INDEX	64	312	1	0	8	0	
9	AURORAJISUTILTY$	SNS$REFADDR_INDEX	INDEX	64	291	5	0	8	0	
10	AURORAJISUTILTY$	SNS$SHARED$OBJ_INDEX	INDEX	64	0	0	0	8	0	
11	AURORAJISUTILTY$	SYS_C0011031	INDEX	64	117	1	0	8	0	
12	AURORAJISUTILTY$	SYS_C0011032	INDEX	64	0	0	0	8	0	
13	BILLY	SYS_C0011859	INDEX	128	0	0	0	16	.02	
14	BILLY	SYS_C0011860	INDEX	128	1	1	0	16	.02	
15	BRKADMIN	BROKER_COMMISSION_N1	INDEX	32	0	0	0	4	0	
16	BRKADMIN	BROKER_N1	INDEX	32	20	1	0	4	0	
17	BRKADMIN	CLIENT_N1	INDEX	32	500	8	0	4	0	

Figure 4.9 – Partial output showing index reorganization diagnostics

Seeing index levels beyond four, or bad clustering factors for indexes with supposed high cardinality, should lead you to investigate whether the index should be reorganized or even maintained in the system.

Correcting Space-related Object Performance Problems

While use of locally-managed tablespaces can just about make full tablespace reorganizations a thing of the past, object reorganizations are still necessary to remove headaches like wasted table space, chained/migrated table rows, deep index levels, etc.

Oracle used to leave reorganization capabilities to third party software vendors, but newer versions of the RDBMS engine provide a number of built-in features that allow you to perform object reorganizations with simple DDL commands or packages.

Table 4.3 below summarizes the methods you can use to reorganize your objects when the need arises.

Oracle Version	Object Type	DDL Command/Method	Offline	Online
7.x	Table	Drop/recreate table	Yes	No
	Index	Drop/recreate index	Yes	No
		ALTER INDEX REBUILD	Yes	No
8.0	Table	Drop/recreate table	Yes	No
	Table Partition	Drop/recreate table	Yes	No
	Index	Drop/recreate index	Yes	No
		ALTER INDEX REBUILD	Yes	No
	Index Partition	ALTER INDEX REBUILD PARTITION	Yes	No
8.1	Heap Table	Drop/recreate table	Yes	No
		ALTER TABLE MOVE	Yes	No
	Table Partition	ALTER TABLE MOVE PARTITION	Yes	No
	Index-Organized table	ALTER TABLE MOVE	Yes	Yes
	Index	Drop/recreate index	Yes	No
		ALTER INDEX REBUILD*	Yes	Yes
	Index Partition	ALTER INDEX REBUILD PARTITION*	Yes	Yes
9.x	Heap Table	Drop/recreate table	Yes	No
		ALTER TABLE MOVE	Yes	No
		Online Table Redefinition	NA	Yes
	Table Partition	ALTER TABLE MOVE PARTITION	Yes	No
	Index-Organized table	ALTER TABLE MOVE	Yes	Yes
	Index	Drop/recreate index	Yes	No
		ALTER INDEX REBUILD*	Yes	Yes
	Index Partition	ALTER INDEX REBUILD PARTITION*	Yes	Yes

Table 4.3 – Reorganization methods summary

Note: Restrictions apply as to what indexes can and can't be rebuilt online. Consult the Oracle documentation for specifics.

Reorganizations are just one task that DBAs need to perform periodically, and most include them as part of an overall database maintenance plan.

Database Maintenance Plans

"You can pay me now or pay me later" is a familiar phrase spoken by auto mechanics. Because of time and money (and sometimes just laziness), many folks put off taking their car in for preventative maintenance work.

The thing is, a little work performed over defined intervals in a car's life can really go a long way in ensuring peak performance, as well as stopping those unexpected breakdowns that can really cost a person their time and money.

The same thing is true of a database. Although a database may seem well-tuned and ready to go the first day a production application goes in, over time it can break down (and sometimes break down quickly) unless a DBA periodically performs preventative maintenance to keep it running well.

For the storage diagnostic scripts to accurately perform their calculations, you should set up a maintenance plan that includes periodic updates of dynamic objects' statistics (by using ANALYZE or DBMS_STATS). You should also schedule periodic reorganizations of objects that continually falter because of sub-optimal storage structures.

Only by observing your database over time can you determine the actual timing of such plan runs, but by instituting such scheduled maintenance operations, you can proactively nip any critical problems in the bud before they cause you real pain.

Conclusion

Hopefully, this chapter has convinced you of the importance of having optimized storage structures in your database. Well-designed and organized storage objects can contribute quite a lot to the performance of a database or cause a breakdown that has the potential to cost you a fair amount of downtime.

By using the techniques and scripts in this chapter, you can intelligently plan your space and object layouts so that your storage works for you instead of against you.

In the next chapter, we will look at how the proper use of memory can also make or break your database's performance capabilities.

Chapter 5

Maximizing Memory

When the subject of Oracle performance tuning comes up, almost every database professional thinks of tweaking the RAM memory settings.

After all, don't servers with more RAM run faster than comparable servers with less memory?

Shouldn't databases work the same?

Not surprisingly, the general answer is yes. Databases operating with more memory will usually run hundreds of times faster than those whose RAM allocations are rationed out in smaller portions. There are, of course, exceptions to every rule, and those will be covered in this chapter.

Those who think that throwing memory at a database is always going to solve serious performance problems are setting themselves up for a rude awakening. It takes a careful blend of balance and investigation to determine exactly how much memory a database needs and where those allocations should be made.

It is also critically important not to over allocate a database's memory allotment. Doing so can cause a server to page swap and thrash to a point where all operations come to a complete standstill.

Without a doubt, a small book could be written on the subject of memory concepts and tuning within Oracle.

Instead of trying to cover every nook and cranny with respect to memory optimization, this chapter will focus on getting the most bang for the buck when you begin to turn Oracle's memory knobs.

There is nothing more irritating than spending an hour and a half reading an in-depth white paper on something like Oracle latch analysis (that provides numerous graphs and a bibliography the size of your arm), and then discovering that following the author's advice yields no noticeable benefit on the database.

This chapter will work to give you what you need to maximize memory inside and outside your database by focusing on the following topics:

- How to determine if you are giving the right amount of memory to Oracle

- What new memory options in Oracle offer the most potential for improving performance

- How to keep data, code, and object definitions in memory so response times are the fastest possible

- How to quickly pinpoint user sessions that degrade response times by using excessive memory resources

Once you understand these things, you will be in a better position to ensure that your Oracle database is properly configured from a memory standpoint. To begin, you need to analyze the current memory configuration and usage of the database.

Getting a Handle on Memory Usage

Not surprisingly, each release of Oracle has featured additional memory parameters that can be tweaked to create an optimal memory configuration for your database. And in trained hands, these parameters can make a dramatic difference in how well your database runs.

Happily, Oracle has now made these key memory settings dynamic in version 9i and above, meaning that DBAs can now size their SGA without having to start and stop the database.

The starting point with an existing database is to understand how much RAM your database server offers, and then determine the current settings of the Oracle SGA. This provides a basis for judging whether Oracle can benefit from adding or manipulating memory and how much headroom exists.

Obtaining the memory configuration of your server will depend on the hardware/operating system platform. Most operating systems have decent GUI interfaces that allow for such configuration information to be obtained through pointing and clicking.

Once you know the memory amounts for the server, you should perform diagnostics (or ask your system administrator to do them) to investigate the metrics of the paging/swapping situation on the server. Again, getting such information will depend on your hardware platform. However, regardless of the platform, you want to avoid excessive paging and swapping. They tend to degrade the overall performance of anything that runs on the server, since data is constantly transferred from RAM to physical swap files and then back again.

After you have a comfort level for the memory behavior on the database server, you will need to turn your attention to Oracle. The first step is to find the size of the current SGA that controls the database. To get such information, you can use the *sgasize.sql* script. Note that this script can be used on all Oracle versions. However, some of the columns may be NULL or zero because certain memory regions are not available in all versions.

sgasize.sql

```
select
        db_size_in_mb - db_caches db_buffers_in_mb,
        db_caches db_caches_mb,
        fixed_size_in_mb,
        lb_size_in_mb,
        sp_size_in_mb,
        lp_size_in_mb,
        jp_size_in_mb
from
(select
        round (max(a.bytes) / 1024 / 1024, 2)  db_size_in_mb
  from
        sys.v_$sgastat a
 where
        (a.name = 'db_block_buffers' or a.name = 'buffer_cache')),
(select
        nvl(round (sum (b.value) / 1024 / 1024, 2),0) db_caches
  from
        sys.v_$parameter b
 where
        b.name like '%k_cache_size'),
(select
        round (sum (b.bytes) / 1024 / 1024, 2) fixed_size_in_mb
  from
        sys.v_$sgastat b
 where
         b.name = 'fixed_sga'),
(select
        round (sum (c.bytes) / 1024 / 1024, 2) lb_size_in_mb
  from
        sys.v_$sgastat c
 where
```

```
          c.name=  'log_buffer' ),
(select
          round (sum (d.value) / 1024 / 1024, 2) sp_size_in_mb
   from
          sys.v_$parameter d
  where
          d.name = 'shared_pool_size'),
(select
          round (sum (e.value) / 1024 / 1024, 2) lp_size_in_mb
   from
          sys.v_$parameter e
  where
          e.name = 'large_pool_size' ),
(select
          round (sum (f.value) / 1024 / 1024, 2) jp_size_in_mb
   from
          sys.v_$parameter f
  where
          f.name = 'java_pool_size');
```

	DB_BUFFERS_IN_MB	DB_CACHES	FIXED_SIZE_IN_MB	LB_SIZE_IN_MB	SP_SIZE_IN_MB	LP_SIZE_IN_MB	JP_SIZE_IN_MB
1	56	16	.43	.63	48	8	32

Figure 5.1 – Getting a summary of Oracle SGA settings

This script delivers more detailed information than the standard *show sga* command in the server manager or SQL*Plus because it breaks down the standard buffer cache, showing the total amount of memory given to the special 9i and above data caches and displaying information for the large and java pools.

Exactly what each of these areas is and how Oracle uses them is the topic of the next section.

Understanding the SGA

Most DBAs know all about the Oracle System Global Area (SGA). The SGA is Oracle's structural memory area that facilitates the transfer of data and information between clients and the Oracle database. Long gone are the days when only four main tunable components existed. If you are using Oracle9i or above, expect to deal with the following memory regions:

- **Default buffer cache** – This is the default memory cache that stores data blocks when they are read from the database. If the DBA does not specifically place objects in another data cache (which will be covered next), then any data requested by clients from the database will be placed into this cache. This memory area is controlled by the *db_block_buffers* parameter in Oracle8i and below, and *db_cache_size* in Oracle9i and above.

- **Keep buffer cache** - Beginning with Oracle8, a DBA can assign objects to a special cache that will retain those object's requested blocks in RAM for as long as the database is up. The *keep* cache's main function is to hold frequently referenced lookup tables that should always be kept in memory for quick access. The *buffer_pool_keep* parameter controls the size of this cache in Oracle8, while the *db_keep_cache_size* parameter handles the cache in Oracle9i and above. The *keep* pool is a sub-pool of the default buffer cache.

- **Recycle buffer cache** - Imagine the opposite of the *keep* cache, and you have the *recycle* cache. When large table scans occur, the data filling a memory cache is unlikely to be needed again, and should be quickly discarded from RAM. By placing this data into the *recycle* cache, it will neither occupy valuable memory space nor prevent blocks that are needed from being placed in a buffer. However, should it be requested again, the discarded data is quickly available. The *buffer_pool_recycle* parameter controls the size of this cache in Oracle8 and below, while the *db_recycle_cache_size* parameter handles the cache in Oracle9i and above.

- **Specific block size caches** - Beginning in Oracle9i, a DBA can create tablespaces whose blocksize differs from the overall database blocksize. When data is read into the SGA from these tablespaces, their data has to be placed into memory regions that can accommodate their special blocksize. Oracle9i and above has memory settings for 2K, 4K, 8K, 16K, and 32K caches. The configuration parameter names are in the pattern of *db_nk_cache_size*.

- **Shared pool** - This familiar area holds object structures and code definitions, as well as other metadata. Setting the proper amount of memory in the shared pool assists a great deal in improving overall performance with respect to code execution and object references. The *shared_pool_size* parameter controls this memory region.

- **Large pool** – Starting in Oracle8, a DBA can configure an optional, specialized memory region called the large pool, that holds items for shared server operations, backup and restore tasks, and other miscellaneous things. The *large_pool_size* parameter controls this memory region. The large pool is also used for sorting when the multi-threaded server (MTS) is implemented.

- **Java pool** – This area handles the memory for Java methods, class definitions, etc. The *java_pool_size* parameter controls the amount of memory for this area.

- **Redo log buffer** - This area buffers modifications that are made to the database before they are physically written to the redo log files. The *log_buffer* configuration parameter controls this memory area.

Note that Oracle also maintains a "fixed" area in the SGA that contains a number of atomic variables, pointers, and other miscellaneous structures that reference areas of the SGA.

Gaining Insight into Memory Use

Once you understand the current settings of your SGA, you should then turn your attention to how well it is being utilized. You can use a number of key ratios and wait metrics to assemble a global picture of SGA performance.

Before you use the scripts below to obtain key memory metrics, you should be aware that some database professionals passionately believe that ratio-based analysis is a worthless endeavor, and only favor a wait-based or bottleneck approach instead. There are certainly valid reasons for not relying solely on ratios to determine if your database is functioning properly.

However, when practiced correctly, ratio-based analysis is indeed worthwhile and can contribute to your understanding of system performance. The chapter about ratio-based and bottleneck analysis provides more information on this topic.

That said, what are some of the key indicators of memory efficiency and usage? Rather than list each metric in a single script, the *memsnap.sql* script below obtains many key memory metrics in a single query and presents them all at once.

memsnap.sql

```
select
        buffer_hit_ratio,
        percent_shared_pool_free,
        lib_cache_hit_ratio,
        object_reloads,
        dd_cache_hit_ratio,
        redo_log_space_waits,
        redo_log_space_wait_time,
        mem_sort_ratio,
        parse_execute_ratio,
        buffer_busy_waits,
        latch_miss_ratio
from
(select
        100 -
        100 *
        (round ((sum (decode (name, 'physical reads', value, 0)) -
         sum (decode (name, 'physical reads direct', value, 0)) -
         sum (decode (name,
         'physical reads direct (lob)', value, 0))) /
         (sum (decode (name,
         'session logical reads', value, 1))),3)) buffer_hit_ratio
 from
        sys.v_$sysstat
 where
         name in ('session logical reads',
                  'physical reads direct (lob)',
                  'physical reads', 'physical reads direct')),
(select
        round (100 * (free_bytes / shared_pool_size), 2)
        percent_shared_pool_free
  from
        (select
                sum (bytes) free_bytes
           from
                sys.v_$sgastat
          where
                name = 'free memory'
            and
                pool = 'shared pool'),
        (select
                value shared_pool_size
           from
                sys.v_$parameter
          where
                name = 'shared_pool_size')),
(select
        100 - round ((sum (reloads) /
        sum (pins)) * 100, 2) lib_cache_hit_ratio
  from
        sys.v_$librarycache),
(select
        100 - round ((sum (getmisses) /
```

```sql
          (sum (gets) + sum (getmisses)) * 100), 2) dd_cache_hit_ratio
from    sys.v_$rowcache),
(select round (
          (100 * b.value) /
          decode ((a.value + b.value), 0, 1, (a.value + b.value)),
          2)mem_sort_ratio
  from
        v$sysstat a,
        v$sysstat b
 where
        a.name = 'sorts (disk)'
   and b.name = 'sorts (memory)'),
(select
        round(100 * (sum (sys.v_$latch.misses) /
        sum (sys.v_$latch.gets)),2) latch_miss_ratio
  from
        sys.v_$latch),
(select
        round (100 * (a.value - b.value) /
        decode (a.value, 0, 1, a.value), 2) parse_execute_ratio
  from
        sys.v_$sysstat a,
        sys.v_$sysstat b
 where
        a.name = 'execute count'
   and b.name = 'parse count (hard)'),
(select
        nvl(sum(total_waits),0) buffer_busy_waits
from
        sys.v_$system_event a,
        sys.v_$event_name b
where
        a.event = 'buffer busy waits' and
        a.event (+) = b.name),
(select
        sum(reloads) object_reloads
  from
        sys.v_$librarycache),
(select
        value redo_log_space_waits
  from
        sys.v_$sysstat
where
        name = 'redo log space requests'),
(select
        value redo_log_space_wait_time
  from
        sys.v_$sysstat
where
        name = 'redo log space wait time');
```

BUFFER_HIT_RATIO	LIB_CACHE_HIT_RATIO	OBJECT_RELOADS	DD_CACHE_HIT_RATIO	MEM_SORT_RATIO	PARSE_EXECUTE_RATIO	PERCENT_SHARED_POOL_FREE
1	99.9	99.99	9	94.93	99.89	98.12	69.33

Figure 5.2 – Partial output showing key memory usage metrics

The buffer cache hit ratio is the first statistic shown in the above script. As mentioned, many DBAs today maintain that this measure is not a good indicator of performance, but is this actually true?

The Buffer Cache Hit Ratio – Still Worthwhile?

The buffer cache hit ratio indicates how often data is found in memory vs. disk. Critics of this ratio complain that it is not a good indicator of performance because (a) many analysts use cumulative numbers for the computations, which can artificially inflate the value to a meaningless measure, and (b) it does not negatively reflect excessive logical I/O activity, which, although faster than disk I/O, can certainly suppress performance on any database.

These complaints have merit. One must use delta statistics over time to come up with a meaningful value for the ratio, and high logical I/O values can definitely be a leading cause of bad execution times. However, when properly computed, the buffer cache hit ratio is an excellent indicator of how often the data requested by users is found in RAM instead of disk, a fact of no small importance.

The global statistic shown above is a good place to start, but you do not have to stop there. You can penetrate deeper to find cache hit ratios at the buffer pool, session, and SQL statement level.
If you use a *keep* and *recycle* buffer pool in addition to the default buffer cache, you can use the *poolhit.sql* script to find the hit rates in each pool:

poolhit.sql

```
select
        name,
        100 * (1 - (physical_reads / (db_block_gets +
        consistent_gets))) hit_ratio
from
        sys.v$buffer_pool_statistics
where
        db_block_gets + consistent_gets > 0;
```

Output from the above query might look like the following:

```
NAME        HIT_RATIO
----------  ---------
DEFAULT         92.82
KEEP            93.98
RECYCLE         85.05
```

From the overall buffer caches, you can turn to the cache hit ratios for user processes. The *sesshitrate.sql* script below will provide you with a buffer cache hit ratio for all currently connected sessions:

sesshitrate.sql

```
select
        b.sid sid,
        decode (b.username,null,e.name,b.username)
        user_name,
        d.spid os_id,
        b.machine machine_name,
        to_char(logon_time,'mm/dd/yy hh:mi:ss pm')
        logon_time,
        100 - 100 *
        (round ((sum (decode (c.name,
        'physical reads', value, 0)) -
        sum (decode (c.name,
        'physical reads direct', value, 0)) -
        sum(decode (c.name,
        'physical reads direct (lob)', value, 0))) /
        (sum (decode (c.name,
        'db block gets', value, 1)) +
        sum (decode (c.name,
        'consistent gets', value, 0))),3)) hit_ratio
from
        sys.v_$sesstat a,
        sys.v_$session b,
        sys.v_$statname c,
        sys.v_$process d,
```

```
        sys.v_$bgprocess e
where
        a.statistic#=c.statistic# and
        b.sid=a.sid   and
        d.addr = b.paddr and
        e.paddr (+) = b.paddr   and
        c.name in ('physical reads',
                    'physical reads direct',
                    'physical writes direct (lob)',
                    'physical reads direct (lob)',
                    'db block gets',
                    'consistent gets')
group by
        b.sid,
        d.spid,
        decode (b.username,null,e.name,b.username),
        b.machine,
        to_char(logon_time,'mm/dd/yy hh:mi:ss pm')
order by
        6 desc;
```

	SID	USER_NAME	OS_ID	MACHINE_NAME	LOGON_TIME	HIT_RATIO
1	1	PMON	292	EBT2K11	01/03/03 01:01:16 pm	100
2	2	DBW0	1148	EBT2K11	01/03/03 01:01:16 pm	100
3	3	LGWR	304	EBT2K11	01/03/03 01:01:16 pm	100
4	6	RECO	1136	EBT2K11	01/03/03 01:01:17 pm	100
5	8	SYS	2552	EBT2K\BILLYWS	01/17/03 02:59:01 pm	100
6	9	QVIN	2420	EBT2K\BILLYWS	01/17/03 02:39:55 pm	100
7	12	SYSMAN	2948	EBT2K\EBT2K11	01/07/03 10:29:04 am	100
8	14	SYSMAN	2800	EBT2K\EBT2K11	01/07/03 10:29:05 am	100
9	15	SYSMAN	1424	EBT2K\EBT2K11	01/07/03 10:29:05 am	100
10	24	ERADMIN	452	EBT2K\ROBINWS	01/16/03 10:27:14 am	100
11	23	USER21	3176	EBT2K\EBT2K12	01/17/03 03:59:10 pm	100
12	22	SYS	2312	EBT2K\BILLYWS	01/17/03 03:32:51 pm	100
13	21	USER21	2136	EBT2K\EBT2K12	01/14/03 11:12:56 am	100
14	19	SYSMAN	1560	EBT2K\EBT2K11	01/07/03 10:29:05 am	100
15	18	SYS	3972	EBT2K\BILLYWS	01/17/03 03:02:23 pm	100
16	17	SYSMAN	2000	EBT2K\EBT2K11	01/07/03 10:29:05 am	100
17	13	SYSMAN	236	EBT2K\EBT2K11	01/07/03 10:29:05 am	100
18	30	SYS	3752	EBT2K\ROBINWS	01/16/03 09:27:38 am	100
19	29	SYS	3620	EBT2K\BILLYWS	01/17/03 02:57:11 pm	100
20	27	SYS	1884	EBT2K\ROBINWS	01/17/03 03:55:18 pm	100
21	26	SYS	3128	EBT2K\ROBINWS	01/17/03 03:59:45 pm	100
22	11	SYSMAN	2952	EBT2K\EBT2K11	01/07/03 10:29:04 am	100
23	4	CKPT	1176	EBT2K11	01/03/03 01:01:17 pm	100
24	5	SMON	1236	EBT2K11	01/03/03 01:01:17 pm	99.8
25	25	SYSTEM	612	EBT2K\EBT2K11	01/07/03 10:29:44 am	99.5

Figure 5.3 – Sample output showing session hit ratio information

After examining the session hit ratio information, you can move into SQL statement analysis with the *sqlhitrate.sql* script:

sqlhitrate.sql

```
select
        sql_text ,
        b.username ,
        100 - round(100 *
        a.disk_reads/greatest(a.buffer_gets,1),2) hit_ratio
from
        sys.v_$sqlarea a,
        sys.all_users b
where
        a.parsing_user_id=b.user_id and
        b.username not in ('SYS','SYSTEM')
order by
        3 desc;
```

	SQL_TEXT	USERNAME	HIT_RATIO
1	SELECT 1035, COUNT(*) FROM SYS.SEG$ S,SYS.TS$ TS WHERE S.TS# = TS.TS# AND DECODE(BITAND(TS.FLAGS, 3), 1, TO_NUMBER(NULL),S.EXTSIZE	USER1	100
2	COMMIT	QVIN	100
3	SELECT 980, CHAINEDFETCHES,TOTALFETCHES FROM (SELECT VALUE AS CHAINEDFETCHES FROM SYS.V_$SYSSTAT A WHERE NAME='table fetch	USER1	100
4	SELECT 1036, COUNT(*) FROM (SELECT ROUND((100*Sum_Free_Blocks / Sum_Alloc_Blocks),2) PCT_FREE FROM (SELECT Tablespace_Name,SUM(Blocks) Sum_Alloc_Blocks,SUM(bytes) AS Total_space FROM SYS.DBA_DATA_FILES GROUP BY Tablespace_Name), (SELECT	USER1	100
5	SELECT /*+ ALL_ROWS IGNORE_WHERE_CLAUSE */ NVL(SUM(C1),0), NVL(SUM(C2),0), COUNT(DISTINCT C3) FROM (SELECT /*+	QVIN	100
6	COMMIT WORK	QVIN	100
7	/* OracleOEM */ UPDATE smp_vdp_node_info SET status = 'N', DOWN_TIME = :1, DOWN_TIMEZONE = :2 WHERE (status = 'Y') AND (node = :3) AND	SYSMAN	100
8	begin PERFCNTR_DRILLDOWN_QUERIES.fetchcursor_10(QUERY_LIST_IN=>'914',MAX _ROWS_IN=>500,VAR1_OUT=>:R001C001,VAR2_OUT=>:R001C002,VAR3_OU	USER1	100
9	SELECT 976, ROUND(A.VALUE/1048576,2) DB,ROUND(B.VALUE/1048576,2) FS,ROUND(C.VALUE/1048576,2) RB,ROUND(D.VALUE/1048576,2) VS FROM	USER1	100
10	LOCK TABLE smp_vdp_node_oms_map IN EXCLUSIVE MODE	SYSMAN	100
11	LOCK TABLE smp_vdg_gateway_map in EXCLUSIVE MODE	SYSMAN	100
12	SELECT 1033, b.USERNAME,b.SID,b.SERIAL#,B.STATUS,DECODE((SUBSTR(B.MACHINE,LENG TH(B.MACHINE),1)),CHR(0),(SUBSTR(B.MACHINE,1,LENGTH(B.MACHINE)-1)),RT RIM(B.MACHINE)) MACHINE,ROUND(SUM(DECODE(c.NAME,'session pga memory',VALUE,0))/1024,2) pga_memory,ROUND(SUM(DECODE(c.NAME,'session uga memory',VALUE,0))/1024,2) uga_memory,ROUND(SUM(DECODE(c.NAME, 'sorts	USER1	100

Figure 5.4 – Sample output showing SQL statement hit ratio analysis

One nuance in the SQL hit ratio script (as well as the buffer pool script, which calculates hit rates for the different buffer pools) that you should be aware of, is that the Oracle *v$sqlarea* view does not provide a way to filter direct reads (physical reads that do not pass through the buffer cache, and consequently do not increment any logical I/O counters). This means it is possible to have a SQL statement that prompts a lot of direct reads, while the hit ratio shows *negative*.

Getting Advice on the Buffer Cache

The old rule of thumb said that if the buffer cache hit ratios were depressed (typically below 90%), you should increase the *db_block_buffer/db_cache_size* parameter until the ratio improved. We have already mentioned that this practice may not yield better overall performance (it will not help excessive logical I/O caused by inefficient SQL calls), but we hasten to add that increasing the cache memory can indeed improve response times for many databases suffering from improper cache sizes.

Of course, memory should be added to Oracle intelligently, which means keeping an eye on server page and swap activity. However, how will you know the amount of extra memory that the cache needs? If the truth were known, most DBAs simply begin edging the memory setting higher with no rhyme or reason, and hope to stop the dial on just the right amount.

With Oracle9i and above, you can use the *db_cache_advice* parameter to help predict the benefit of adding additional memory to the buffer/data cache. Setting this value to ON tells Oracle to begin collecting I/O statistics that can be used to assist you in intelligently assigning additional RAM to Oracle, while not giving more than is actually needed. The technique generally involves setting the *db_cache_advice* parameter to ON during a time that represents the normal workload for the database.

Once the database has been stressed, you can examine the prediction results by using the *cacheadvice.sql* script:

cacheadvice.sql

```
select
       size_for_estimate,
       buffers_for_estimate,
       estd_physical_read_factor,
       estd_physical_reads
from
       sys.v_$db_cache_advice
where
       name = 'DEFAULT'and
       block_size = (select
                            value
                     from
                            sys.v_$parameter
                     where
                            name = 'db_block_size') and
       advice_status = 'ON';
```

	SIZE_FOR_ESTIMATE	BUFFERS_FOR_ESTIMATE	ESTD_PHYSICAL_READ_FACTOR	ESTD_PHYSICAL_READS
1	8	1001	315.959	2718195
2	16	2002	1.6436	14140
3	24	3003	1.2744	10963
4	32	4004	1.0872	9353
5	40	5005	1.0333	8890
6	48	6006	1	8603
7	56	7007	1	8603
8	64	8008	1	8603
9	72	9009	1	8603
10	80	10010	1	8603
11	88	11011	1	8603
12	96	12012	1	8603
13	104	13013	1	8603
14	112	14014	1	8603
15	120	15015	1	8603
16	128	16016	1	8603
17	136	17017	1	8603
18	144	18018	1	8603
19	152	19019	1	8603
20	160	20020	1	8603

Figure 5.5 – Examining Oracle's prediction for adding or subtracting RAM from the data cache

In the above example, Oracle is telling us that for this small 9.2 instance, anything above 16MB for the buffer cache will be wasted RAM.

As a general guideline, all memory available on the host should be tuned, and the *db_cache_size* should be allocating RAM resources up to the point of diminishing returns (Figure 5.6). This is the point where additional buffer blocks do not significantly improve the buffer hit ratio.

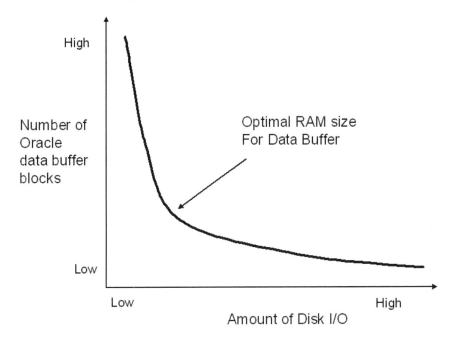

Figure 5.6- The optimal size of the RAM data buffer

The new *v$db_cache_advice* view is similar to an Oracle7 utility that also predicted the benefit of adding data buffers. The Oracle7 utility used the *x$kcbrbh* view to track buffer hits and the *x$kcbcbh* view to track buffer misses.

How to Keep Data Where You Want It

You definitely want to keep frequently accessed data in the buffer/data cache, so that queries needing that data have the fastest possible access to it. How can you accomplish this?

If you are on Oracle version 7, you can utilize the *cache* property of a table, which specifies that any blocks retrieved from the table during a table scan be placed at the most recently used end of the LRU list in the cache. This does not mean that they will remain in the cache forever, but at least you are giving the blocks a fighting chance to stay in the cache over other data blocks. An example of enabling the *cache* property for a table named ERADMIN.ADMISSION would be:

```
alter table eradmin.admission cache;
```

With Oracle version 8 and above, there is a better option. You can enable the *keep* pool, a specialized area carved out of the overall buffer/data cache that allows you to retain needed data blocks on a more permanent basis. The *buffer_pool_keep* parameter controls the size of this cache in Oracle8, while the *db_keep_cache_size* parameter handles this cache allotment in Oracle9i and above. While you do not have to do any special cache sizing to enable the *cache* property of a table, using the *keep* pool entails some planning with respect to how much data you want to pin in memory.

An example of placing a table named ERADMIN.ADMISSION into the keep pool would be:

```
alter table eradmin.admission storage(buffer_pool keep);
```

As you might have already surmised, small objects and lookup tables are the best candidates for placement in the *keep* buffer pool or for enabling their *cache* property.

However, there are other caches you can use to enhance the performance of your database as well.

Exploiting the New 9i Data Caches

In Oracle9i and above, you can create tablespaces with blocksizes that differ from the overall database blocksize. If you choose to do this, then you must also enable one or more of the new *db_nk_cache_size* parameters, so that blocks read in from tablespaces that have a different blocksize than the regular database blocksize have a cache to reside.

For example, if you create a tablespace with a 16K blocksize, then you must also set aside RAM for those blocks using the *db_16k_cache_size* parameter. Note that such allocations are in addition to the memory allotments specified by the *db_cache_size* parameter.

This feature allows you to tune your database in ways that were impossible in earlier versions of Oracle. For example, you can use the large (16-32K) blocksize data caches to store data from indexes or tables that are the object of repeated large scans. Does such a thing really help performance? A small but revealing test can answer that question.

For the test, the following query will be used against a 9i database that has a database block size of 8K, but also has the 16K cache enabled along with a 16K tablespace:

```
select
      count(*)
from
      eradmin.admission
where
      patient_id between 1 and 40000;
```

The ERADMIN.ADMISSION table has 150,000 rows in it and has an index build on the PATIENT_ID column. An EXPLAIN of the query reveals that it uses an index range scan to produce the desired end result:

```
Execution Plan
----------------------------------------------------------
   0      SELECT STATEMENT Optimizer=CHOOSE
   1      (Cost=41 Card=1 Bytes=4)
   1    0    SORT (AGGREGATE)
   2    1      INDEX (FAST FULL SCAN) OF 'ADMISSION_PATIENT_ID'
                (NON-UNIQUE) (Cost=41 Card=120002 Bytes=480008)
```

Executing the query (twice to eliminate parse activity and to cache any data) with the index residing in a standard 8K tablespace produces these runtime statistics:

```
Statistics
----------------------------------------------------------
        0   recursive calls
        0   db block gets
      421   consistent gets
        0   physical reads
        0   redo size
      371   bytes sent via SQL*Net to client
      430   bytes received via SQL*Net from client
        2   SQL*Net roundtrips to/from client
        0   sorts (memory)
        0   sorts (disk)
        1   rows processed
```

To test the effectiveness of the new 16K cache and 16K tablespace, the index used by the query will be rebuilt into the larger tablespace, while everything else remains the same:

```
alter index
    eradmin.admission_patient_id
    rebuild nologging noreverse tablespace indx_16k;
```

Once the index is nestled firmly into the 16K tablespace, the query is re-executed (again, twice) with the following runtime statistics being produced:

```
Statistics
----------------------------------------------------
        0  recursive calls
        0  db block gets
      211  consistent gets
        0  physical reads
        0  redo size
      371  bytes sent via SQL*Net to client
      430  bytes received via SQL*Net from client
        2  SQL*Net roundtrips to/from client
        0  sorts (memory)
        0  sorts (disk)
        1  rows processed
```

As you can see, the amount of logical reads has been cut in half simply by using the new 16K tablespace and accompanying 16K data cache. Clearly, the benefits of the proper use of the new data caches and multi-block tablespace features of Oracle9i are worth investigating and testing in your own database.

Other Interesting Buffer Cache Metrics

If you want a deeper understanding of how the buffer cache is being utilized, there are a few additional queries you can run to gain such insight. If the *keep* and *recycle* buffer caches are being used, you can run the *cacheobjcnt.sql* query to get an idea on how many objects have been assigned to each cache:

cacheobjcnt.sql

```
select
      decode(cachehint, 0, 'default', 1,
      'keep', 2, 'recycle', null) cache,
      count(*) objects
from
      sys.seg$ s
where
      s.user#  in
      (select
          user#
       from
          sys.user$
       where
          name not in ('sys','system'))
group by
      decode(cachehint, 0, 'default', 1,
      'keep', 2, 'recycle', null)
order by
    1;
```

Output may resemble something like the following:

```
CACHE       OBJECTS
-----------------
default      2023
keep            5
```

Finally, you may wish to analyze the buffer cache activity from time to time to see how it is being utilized. The *buffutl.sql* script will show you how full the cache currently is along with the state of the buffers in the cache:

buffutl.sql

```
select
      'free' buffer_state,
      nvl(sum(blocksize) / 1024 ,0) amt_kb
from
      sys.x$bh a,
      sys.ts$ b
where
      state = 0  and
      a.ts#  =  b.ts#
union all
select
      'read/mod' buffer_state,
      nvl(sum(blocksize) / 1024 ,0) amt_kb
from
```

```
        sys.x$bh a,
        sys.ts$ b
where
        state = 1  and
        a.ts#  =  b.ts#
union all
select
        'read/notmod',
        nvl(sum(blocksize) / 1024 ,0) amt_kb
from
        sys.x$bh a,
        sys.ts$ b
where
        state = 2  and
        a.ts#  =  b.ts#
union all
select
        'being read' buffer_state,
        nvl(sum(blocksize) / 1024 ,0) amt_kb
from
        sys.x$bh a,
        sys.ts$ b
where
        state = 3  and
        a.ts#  =  b.ts#
order by
        1;
```

Output from the above query might look something like this:

```
BUFFER_STATE       AMT_KB
-----------------------
being read           5920
free                23568
read/mod            47952
read/notmod             0
```

Now that you have a good understanding of how to interrogate the buffer cache, the next area you'll want to examine is the shared pool.

Looking into the Shared Pool

The four metrics below are revealed by the *memsnap.sql* query (after the buffer cache hit ratio), and concern the shared pool. Execution response times can be adversely affected if Oracle has to handle parse activity, perform object definition lookups, or manage other code-related or reference tasks.

The shared pool helps Oracle keep these reference-related activities to a minimum by holding SQL statements, along with code and object definitions, in memory.

As with the data cache, properly sizing the shared pool can be tricky and often involves trial and error. The *memsnap.sql* query reveals that a shared pool that is sized too small has the following characteristics:

- Zero or near-zero percent free in the pool after the database has only been up a short while

- A library cache hit ratio that is below average (95% or below)

- Many object reloads (due to definitions being forced from the pool prematurely)

- A below average data dictionary cache hit ratio (95% or below)

The last three metrics mentioned above should be viewed in the same light as the buffer cache hit ratio, in that delta measurements often produce more meaningful results than cumulative measurements, and some databases will perform quite well with measures that appear non-optimal.

With respect to the percent free in the shared pool, a near zero reading after the database has been up for some time is probably fine. But, if the pool drops to zero free shortly after Oracle is started, you have a strong indication that it may be sized too small.

When Does Less Become More?

So, why not just size the shared pool to some huge number and be done? First, as with sizing the data cache, you should keep an eye on available memory at the server level, so that paging or swapping is not induced when RAM is added to the shared pool.

However, the main reason you do not want to oversize the shared pool is that sometimes a large pool actually causes *reduced* response times. How can this happen? The simple explanation is that it takes Oracle longer to search for object definitions or SQL statements in a shared pool that is gargantuan.

Oracle will always try and reuse SQL statements to keep from re-parsing a query, and while this can certainly reduce execution times when a shared pool is sized correctly, it can actually hinder progress when the pool is so large that Oracle wastes time interrogating it.

Getting More Details on Shared Pool Usage

While the global ratios and metrics can provide a rough idea of how efficient the shared pool is, looking deeper will provide more details on how the pool is being utilized and whether it is sized correctly.

The two main areas of the shared pool are the library and data dictionary caches. The library cache holds commonly used SQL statements, basically database code objects. One excellent method of improving performance in Oracle is to encourage the reuse of SQL statements, so that expensive parse operations are avoided. The library cache assists this tuning effort.

The data dictionary cache enables the sharing of object definition information. The dictionary cache stores the description of database structures, so that needed structure references can be resolved as quickly as possible.

There are three queries you can use to extract the details of library cache usage. The *libdet.sql* script will show you which object types are taking longer to find than others:

libdet.sql

```
select
        namespace,
        gets,
        round(gethitratio*100,2) gethitratio,
        pins,
        round(pinhitratio*100,2) pinhitratio,
        reloads,
        invalidations
from
        sys.v_$librarycache
order by
        1;
```

	NAMESPACE	GETS	GETHITRATIO	PINS	PINHITRATIO	RELOADS	INVALIDATIONS
1	BODY	7755	99.47	7761	99.34	0	0
2	CLUSTER	9962	99.84	6838	99.62	0	0
3	INDEX	682	54.99	408	20.34	0	0
4	JAVA DATA	16	62.5	61	73.77	2	0
5	JAVA RESOURCE	0	100	0	100	0	0
6	JAVA SOURCE	16	81.25	22	50	2	0
7	OBJECT	0	100	0	100	0	0
8	PIPE	0	100	0	100	0	0
9	SQL AREA	2491828	99.56	11586427	99.8	1039	5494
10	TABLE/PROCEDURE	499978	99	3052161	99.64	1338	0
11	TRIGGER	44032	99.92	44039	99.91	0	0

Figure 5.7 – Extracting the library cache details

You can use bottleneck or wait-based analysis in addition to ratios and drill down queries to get an idea of overall library cache health.

The *libwait.sql* query provides clues about whether Oracle has been waiting for library cache activities:

```
select
       b.name,
       nvl(max(a.total_waits),0)
from
       sys.v_$system_event a,
       sys.v_$event_name b
where
       a.event (+)  = b.name and
       b.name in ('latch free','library cache load lock',
                  'library cache lock','library cache pin')
group by
       b.name
```

Output from the above script might resemble the following:

```
NAME                          WAITS
----------------------------------
latch free                       16
library cache load lock           2
library cache lock                0
library cache pin                 0
```

Seeing increasing numbers of waits for the above events could indicate an undersized shared pool.

You can dig even deeper into the library cache and uncover exactly which objects currently reside in the cache.

The *libobj.sql* script will show you everything you need to know on this front, but be forewarned, as this script can return large amounts of data in databases with large shared pools and many references to code and data objects:

libobj.sql

```
select
        owner,
        name,
        type,
        sharable_mem,
        loads,
        executions,
        locks,
        pins,
        kept
from
        sys.v_$db_object_cache
order by
        type asc;
```

	OWNER	NAME	TYPE	SHARABLE_MEM	LOADS
8	[NULL]	select i.obj#, i.flags, u.name, o.name from sys.obj$ o, sys.user$ u, ind$ idx, sys.indpart$ i	CURSOR	11416	1
9	[NULL]	select /*+ rule */ bucket_cnt, row_cnt, cache_cnt, null_cnt, timestamp#, sample_size, minimum,	CURSOR	10468	1
10	[NULL]	select i.obj#, i.flags, u.name, o.name from sys.obj$ o, sys.user$ u, ind$ idx, sys.indpart$ i	CURSOR	1064	1
11	[NULL]	select /*+ rule */ bucket_cnt, row_cnt, cache_cnt, null_cnt, timestamp#, sample_size, minimum,	CURSOR	1068	1
12	[NULL]	select grantee#,privilege#,nvl(col#,0),max(nvl(opti	CURSOR	1003	1
13	[NULL]	SELECT 1 FROM SYS.OBJ$ WHERE OWNER# =1	CURSOR	920	1
14	[NULL]	select privilege#,nvl(col#,0),max(nvl(option$,0))fro	CURSOR	982	1
15	[NULL]	select signature from triggerjavas$ where obj#=:1	CURSOR	4224	1
16	[NULL]	select class_name, class_factory, class_factory_	CURSOR	966	1
17	[NULL]	select class_name, class_factory, class_factory_	CURSOR	5516	1
18	[NULL]	select flags from triggerjavaf$ where obj#=:1	CURSOR	903	1
19	[NULL]	select flags from triggerjavaf$ where obj#=:1	CURSOR	4524	1
20	[NULL]	select text from view$ where rowid=:1	CURSOR	895	1
21	[NULL]	select text from view$ where rowid=:1	CURSOR	4252	1
22	[NULL]	select privilege#,nvl(col#,0),max(nvl(option$,0))fro	CURSOR	6848	1
23	[NULL]	SELECT 1 FROM SYS.OBJ$ WHERE OWNER# =1	CURSOR	6960	1
24	[NULL]	insert into uet$ (segfile#,segblock#,ext#,ts#,file#,b	CURSOR	5756	1
25	[NULL]	select count (*), state from SYSTEM.DEF$_AQER	CURSOR	940	1

Figure 5.8 - Drilling down into the library cache

How to Keep Code Where You Want It

Using the above script, you can see how often an object has been loaded into the cache. Many loads could indicate that the object is continuously being forced from the cache, which would potentially degrade performance.

If the object is a code object such as a procedure, package, etc., you can pin the code in the cache to stop it from being removed. In the above query, you can reference the *kept* column to see which code objects (if any) have already been pinned.

The *dbms_shared_pool* package is used to pin or unpin code objects to and from the library cache. For example, if you had a frequently referenced procedure called *ERADMIN.ADD_ADMISSION,* and you wanted to make sure that it would always be found in the library cache for quick reference, you would execute the following:

```
exec sys.dbms_shared_pool.keep('ERADMIN.ADD_ADMISSION','P');
```

Performing a pin keeps the code where you want it at all times. Pinned objects are also impervious to an *alter system flush shared_pool* command.

While this technique works well for code objects, what about regular SQL statements? How can you keep them in the shared pool so that parse operations are minimized? The easiest method is to ensure that user sessions are launching identical SQL statements, which allows reuse to occur in the cache.

If Oracle detects that a user process has launched an identical SQL statement that is already present in the cache, it will reuse the statement rather than parse and load it into memory. Using literals in SQL statements instead of bind variables can greatly hinder this process from occurring. Again, the key to statement reuse is that the SQL has to be *identical,* and the use of literals in SQL statements can entirely negate this.

If you are not able to encase your user's SQL in applications or stored code objects to ensure bind variables are being used instead of literals, what do you do? In version 8.1.6, Oracle quietly introduced the *cursor_sharing* parameter, which can deal with the problem of literals in otherwise identical SQL statements in a hurry.

If you set this parameter to *force*, Oracle will substitute bind variables in the place of literals in any SQL statement and place it into the library cache. This permits any statement submitted subsequently to be reused, so long as the only difference is its bind variable(s).

Is there anything else you should look into with respect to the shared pool? One other area of interest is the data dictionary cache.

More Shared Pool Metrics

To see how often Oracle is finding the system references it needs in the data dictionary; you can use the *dictdet.sql* script, which is sorted from best-hit ratio to worst:

dictdet.sql

```
select
        parameter,
        usage,
        gets,
        getmisses,
        100 - round((getmisses/
        (gets + getmisses) * 100),2) hit_ratio
from
        sys.v_$rowcache
where
        gets + getmisses <> 0
order by
        5 desc;
```

	PARAMETER	USAGE	GETS	GETMISSES	HIT_RATIO
1	dc_profiles	1	37318	1	100
2	dc_tablespaces	20	287977	20	99.99
3	dc_users	39	393939	42	99.99
4	dc_rollback_segments	12	106272	11	99.99
5	dc_user_grants	36	172771	48	99.97
6	dc_files	14	35355	14	99.96
7	dc_usernames	18	94137	35	99.96
8	dc_sequences	5	3426	18	99.48
9	dc_global_oids	19	1477	19	98.73
10	dc_tablespace_quotas	14	974	16	98.38
11	dc_object_ids	1037	82692	1521	98.19
12	dc_segments	629	41262	916	97.83
13	dc_objects	1638	77893	4367	94.69
14	dc_histogram_defs	1262	19592	2241	89.74
15	dc_constraints	1	1482	748	66.46
16	dc_table_scns	0	6	6	50

Figure 5.9 - Drilling down into the dictionary cache

Just as with the library cache, a high data dictionary cache hit ratio is desirable. You should strive for a hit ratio between 90 - 100%, with 95% being a good rule-of-thumb benchmark.

Note that when a database is first started, the overall data dictionary cache hit ratio, as well as the individual hit ratios in the above query, will not be at an optimal level. This is because all references to object definitions will be relatively new, and as such, must be placed into the shared pool. Look for hit ratios between eighty and ninety percent for new database startups.

If, however, after a solid hour or two of steady database time, the data dictionary cache hit ratio has not increased to desirable levels, you should look into the possibility of increasing the *shared_pool_size* parameter.

While there is certainly more that can be discussed regarding shared pools, the areas covered above are the normal hot spots. Are there any other SGA issues that should be checked periodically? One area is the redo log buffer.

Examining the Log Buffer

Sometimes a user process must wait for space in the redo log buffer. Oracle uses the log buffer to cache redo entries prior to writing them to disk, and if the buffer area is not large enough for the redo entry load, waits can occur.

The log buffer is normally small in comparison with other regions of the SGA, and a small increase in size can significantly enhance throughput.

The *memsnap.sql* script contains two main numbers to watch for the log buffer, which are:

- redo log space requests and (maybe more importantly)
- redo log wait time

If either statistic strays too far from 0, then you may want to increase the *log_buffer* parameter and add more memory to the redo log buffer.

Once you have a handle on how the SGA is performing globally, you might want to look into memory usage at the session level to see which processes are consuming the most resources and making life miserable for everyone.

Investigating Session Memory Usage

It is not uncommon for one or two users to cause runtime problems that plague an entire database. The problem could be a runaway process, an untuned batch procedure, or other user-initiated operation. Oftentimes, user connection memory consumption can get out of hand, and extreme cases can cause headaches at both the database and operating system level (ORA-4030 errors).

Please remember that the session memory issue only applies when you are not using the Oracle multi-threaded server (MTS). If you implement the MTS, Oracle will allocate all SGA sort areas to the large pool, and your sessions will not have external PGA memory regions.

If your database server does not have an overabundance of memory, then periodically you should check to see who the heavy memory users are, along with the total percentage of memory each user consumes.

If you see one or two users who have more than 15-50% of the total memory usage, then you should investigate the sessions further to see the kind of activities they are performing.

You can use the *memhog.sql* script to find the sessions that use the most memory in a database:

memhog.sql

```
select
      sid,
      username,
      round(total_user_mem/1024,2) mem_used_in_kb,
      round(100 * total_user_mem/total_mem,2) mem_percent
```

```
from
(select
    b.sid sid,
    nvl(b.username,p.name) username,
    sum(value) total_user_mem
from
    sys.v_$statname c,
    sys.v_$sesstat a,
    sys.v_$session b,
    sys.v_$bgprocess p
where
    a.statistic#=c.statistic# and
    p.paddr (+) = b.paddr and
    b.sid=a.sid and
    c.name in ('session pga memory','session uga memory')
group by
    b.sid, nvl(b.username,p.name)),
(select
    sum(value) total_mem
from
    sys.v_$statname c,
    sys.v_$sesstat a
where
    a.statistic#=c.statistic# and
    c.name in ('session pga memory','session uga memory'))
order by
    3 desc;
```

	SID	USERNAME	MEM_USED_IN_KB	MEM_PERCENT
1	2	DBW0	740.92	18.28
2	14	SYS	685.63	16.91
3	7	SNP0	417.76	10.31
4	3	LGWR	295.21	7.28
5	5	SMON	275.42	6.79
6	13	SYS	232.14	5.73
7	8	SNP1	217.38	5.36
8	11	SNP4	216.77	5.35
9	9	SNP2	200.73	4.95
10	10	SNP3	200.73	4.95
11	12	DBSNMP	188.45	4.65
12	4	CKPT	172.29	4.25
13	6	RECO	150.95	3.72
14	22	SYS	86.88	2.14
15	1	PMON	76.39	1.88

Figure 5.10 – Sample output showing the top memory users in a database

Another metric shown in the *memsnap.sql* script is the parse to execute ratio. It shows the percentage of SQL executed that did not incur a hard parse. Seeing low values might indicate that users are executing SQL with many hard-coded literals instead of bind variables within the application. High values (90% +) generally indicate Oracle is saving precious CPU resources by avoiding heavy parse tasks.

While the above figures help you get a handle on session memory usage within Oracle's program global areas (PGA) and user global areas (UGA), another area you will want to check into is sort activity.

Investigating Sorts

The SGA is not the only memory structure used by Oracle for database work. One of the other memory regions used by Oracle8i and below for normal activity is an area set aside for sort actions. When a sort operation occurs, Oracle attempts to perform the sort in a memory space that exists *at the operating system level.* If the sort is too large to be contained within this space, it will continue the sort on disk - specifically, in the user's assigned temporary tablespace.

Techniques to include in your overall performance strategy are those that relate to minimizing the amount of overall sort activity, and specifically, sort activity that takes place on disk. A good place to start is to understand what things cause sorts in the first place. A list of sort-related commands and SQL-related options include:

- CREATE INDEX, ALTER INDEX ... REBUILD

- DISTINCT

- ORDER BY

- GROUP BY

- UNION

- INTERSECT

- MINUS

- IN, NOT IN

- Certain unindexed joins

- Certain correlated subqueries

All of these SQL commands have the potential to create a sort. As a DBA, you probably will not know which queries will sort entirely in memory and which ones will be forced to go to disk. However, you can get a feel for the overall sort performance by looking at the memory sort ratio that is contained in the output from the *memsnap.sql* query.

As has already been mentioned, when a sort exhausts its memory allotment, it will then be forced to go to disk (the actual place being the user's temporary tablespace assignment). Oracle records the overall number of sorts that are satisfied in memory, as well as those that end up being finalized on disk. Using these numbers, you can calculate the percentage of memory sorts vs. disk sorts and get a feel for how fast your sort activity is being resolved.

If your memory sort ratio falls below 90%, you may want to increase the parameters devoted to memory sorts, *sort_area_size* and *sort_area_retained_size*. Keep in mind that individual users may possess the ability to alter their own sessions and increase their *sort_area_size* assignments. As a DBA, you may want to restrict users that have the *alter session* privilege so that this does not occur.

Oracle9i Sorting

As we have noted, a serious problem in Oracle8i was the requirement that all dedicated connections use a one-size-fits-all *sort_area_size*. Oracle9i now has the option of running automatic PGA memory management.

Oracle has introduced a new Oracle parameter called *pga_aggregate_target*. When the *pga_aggregate_target* parameter is set and you are using dedicated Oracle connections, Oracle9i will ignore all of the PGA parameters in the Oracle file, including *sort_area_size*, *hash_area_size* and *sort_area_retained_size*. Oracle recommends that the value of *pga_aggregate_target* be set to the amount of remaining memory (less a 10 percent overhead for other UNIX tasks) on the UNIX server after the instance has been started.

Once the *pga_aggregate_target* has been set, Oracle will automatically manage PGA memory allocation based upon the individual needs of each Oracle connection. Oracle9i allows the *pga_aggregate_target* parameter to be modified at the instance level with the *alter system* command, thereby allowing the DBA to dynamically adjust the total RAM region available to Oracle9i.

Oracle9i also introduces a new parameter called *workarea_size_policy*. When this parameter is set to automatic, all Oracle connections will benefit from the shared PGA memory. When *workarea_size_policy* is set to manual, connections will allocate memory according to the values for the *sort_area_size* parameter. Under the automatic mode, Oracle tries to maximize the number of work areas that are using optimal memory and uses one-pass memory for the others.

In addition to increasing the amount of memory devoted to sorting, you should also hunt down inefficient SQL that cause needless sorts. For example, *union all* does not cause a sort, whereas *union* does in a SQL query (to eliminate duplicate rows). The *distinct* keyword is oftentimes coded inappropriately (especially by folks transferring from Microsoft Access, which used to use *distinct* for nearly every query).

Miscellaneous Memory Issues

The two final metrics shown in the *memsnap.sql* script deal with buffer busy waits and the latch miss ratio.

Buffer Busy Waits

Buffer busy waits occur when a process needs to access a data block in the buffer cache but cannot because it is being used by another process. So, it must wait. Buffer busy waits normally center around contention for rollback segments, too small an *initrans* setting for tables, or insufficient *freelists* for tables.

The remedy for each situation would be to increase the number of rollback segments, or to alter tables for larger *initrans* settings to allow for more transactions per data block, and more *freelists*. Note that the automatic segment management feature in Oracle9i locally-managed tablespaces can make the *freelist* problem a thing of the past, while the UNDO tablespace feature of 9i can help remedy any rollback contention problem.

However, segment header contention will still occur when concurrent tasks attempt to INSERT into the same table, and multiple *freelists* are required to remove these sources of buffer busy waits.

If you are using Oracle9i and above, you also have a way of finding out what objects have been the source of buffer busy waits. The *bufobjwaits.sql* script will tell you everything you need to know:

---
bufobjwaits.sql

```
select
        owner,
        object_name,
        object_type,
        value waits
from
        sys.v_$segment_statistics
where
        (statistic_name = 'buffer busy waits' and value > 0)
order by
        1,2;


OWNER      OBJECT_NAME    OBJECT_TYPE    WAITS
------------------------------------------------
USR1       TAB1           TABLE              3
USR1       TAB2           TABLE              2
USR1       TAB3           TABLE              2
```

Latches

There have been volumes written about Oracle latches. But, in case you do not know what they are, latches protect the many memory structures in Oracle's SGA. They ensure that one and only one process at a time can run or modify any memory structure at the same instant. Much more

---

restrictive than locks (which at least allow for some collective user interaction), latches have no queuing mechanism, so either you get it or you don't, and you are forced to continually retry if you don't.

Common indicators of latch contention are a latch miss ratio, which records willing-to-wait mode latch requests, and latch immediate miss ratio, which records no-wait mode latch requests.

These statistics reflect how often latch requests were made and satisfied without waiting. If either of these exceeds 1%, then you should drill down further into latching details to identify what latches are responsible for the contention.

To drill down into latch miss details, you can use the *latchdet.sql* script:

latchdet.sql

```
select
        name,
        gets,
        round(misses*100/decode(gets,0,1,gets),2) misses,
        round(spin_gets*100/decode(misses,0,1,misses),2) spins,
        immediate_gets igets,
        round(immediate_misses*100/
        decode(immediate_gets,0,1,immediate_gets),2) imisses,
        sleeps
from
        sys.v_$latch
order by
        2 desc;
```

	NAME	GETS	MISSES	SPINS	IGETS	IMISSES	SLEEPS
1	cache buffers chains	44409592	0	0	4724	0	30
2	cache buffers lru chain	2374631	0	0	0	0	0
3	library cache	572680	.01	0	306	0	155
4	row cache objects	399355	0	0	155	0	52
5	session idle bit	198677	0	0	0	0	0
6	shared pool	164652	0	0	0	0	1
7	enqueues	149031	0	0	0	0	0
8	messages	134876	0	0	0	0	0
9	checkpoint queue latch	82846	0	0	0	0	0
10	redo writing	82507	0	0	0	0	7
11	session allocation	66204	0	0	0	0	0
12	enqueue hash chains	63572	0	0	0	0	0
13	undo global data	29407	0	0	0	0	0
14	redo allocation	23957	.01	0	0	0	8
15	active checkpoint queue latch	20344	0	0	0	0	0
16	session timer	20297	0	0	0	0	0
17	sort extent pool	8813	0	0	0	0	0
18	JOX SGA heap latch	3720	0	0	3120	0	0
19	virtual circuit queues	3046	0	0	0	0	0
20	library cache load lock	2526	0	0	0	0	0
21	cache buffer handles	2453	.08	0	0	0	2
22	shared java pool	2289	0	0	0	0	0
23	transaction allocation	1991	.1	0	0	0	2
24	dml lock allocation	1252	0	0	0	0	0
25	longop free list	998	0	0	0	0	0
26	session switching	983	0	0	0	0	0
27	transaction branch allocation	976	0	0	0	0	0

Figure 5.11 – Output showing latch details

If you want to see whether any sessions are currently waiting for latches, you can use the *currlwaits.sql* script:

currlwaits.sql

```
select
      a.sid,
      username,
      a.event,
      p1text,
      p1,
      p2text,
      p2,
      seq#,
      wait_time,
      state
from
      sys.v_$session_wait a,
```

```
      sys.v_$session b,
      sys.v_$latchname c
where
      a.sid = b.sid and
      a.p2 = c.latch# and
      a.event in
      (select
              name
        from
          sys.v_$event_name
 where
          name like '%latch%')
order by
          1;
```

Keep in mind that catching an actual session latch wait is a difficult thing to do, since they rarely consume much time.

Conclusion

While the general idea that databases run better with more memory is valid, you have to be careful how RAM is distributed to the various memory regions in Oracle for it to be efficiently utilized. By following the points outlined in this chapter, you should be able to:

- Determine how much RAM is currently devoted to the SGA in all your databases

- Quickly get a general snapshot of overall memory usage and efficiency using the *memsnap.sql* script

- Drill down into the data cache and shared pool to determine how well each memory area is being utilized

- Utilize the excellent memory features available in Oracle to make sure that data and code objects are stored where you want them

- Get to the bottom of how each session is using memory on your database

---

As you have seen above, knowing how to properly use memory in Oracle can help cut down on I/O time. The next chapter will explain how to determine where the I/O hotspots are on your systems and how to maximize overall I/O efficiency in your database.

Chapter 6

Pinpointing I/O Hotspots

When complaints begin to surface about your database's performance, oftentimes the root cause can be traced to one or more issues with I/O. The one thing to keep in mind when you begin to monitor the I/O of your database is that you are really reviewing the success of your physical design model.

All the physical storage characteristics and placements, the table and index designs, and the speed with which it all works are on display when I/O is monitored. Because a database's main index of performance is measured by how fast I/O needs are satisfied, it is your responsibility to quickly interrogate Oracle to determine if a reported database slowdown is I/O related.

How can you quickly accomplish such a task? While it is true that every situation is different in some regard, one roadmap you can regularly use is the following:

- Obtain global measures regarding the I/O of your database and note any standout values.

- Examine global statistics regarding how database objects are being accessed.

- Move deeper by examining the I/O of your storage structures and noting where the hotspots appear to be on the disk.

- From storage, uncover what objects appear to be the most in demand.

- If the reported slowdown is currently active, obtain metrics regarding the leading sessions with respect to I/O.

- Once you know what objects and users are responsible for the most I/O issues, drill further into the situation by locating the SQL being issued. We will examine this area more deeply in a subsequent chapter.

Let's walk through each of these steps in detail and see how they can quickly pinpoint the I/O hotspots and bottlenecks in your database.

Global Basic Queries

The first step in unraveling any I/O puzzles in your database is to make a quick check of some of the global database I/O metrics. A query such as the *globiostats.sql* script can be used to get a bird's eye view of a database's I/O:

---
globiostats.sql

```
select
   name,
   value
from
   sys.v_$sysstat
where
   name in
     ('consistent changes',
      'consistent gets',
      'db block changes',
      'db block gets',
      'physical reads',
      'physical writes',
      'sorts (disk)',
      'user commits',
      'user rollbacks'
```

```
    )
  order by
1;
```

Output from the above query might look like the following:

```
NAME                      VALUE
--------------------------------
consistent changes            1
consistent gets           70983
db block changes            243
db block gets               612
physical reads            11591
physical writes              52
sorts (disk)                  0
user commits                 26
user rollbacks                1
```

Although there are some database experts who do not believe the buffer cache hit ratio is of much value anymore (and there are valid reasons for assuming such a stance), you can still perform a cursory check to get an idea of overall disk I/O activity by using the *buffratio.sql* script:

buffratio.sql

```
select
   100 -
   100 *
     (round ((sum (decode (name, 'physical reads',
     value, 0))
       -
     sum (decode (name, 'physical reads direct',
     value, 0)) -
         sum (decode (name,
     'physical reads direct (lob)',
         value, 0))) /
         (sum (decode (name, 'session logical reads',
         value, 1))
          ),3)) hit_ratio
 from
    sys.v_$sysstat
 where
    name in
   ('session logical reads',
    'physical reads direct (lob)',
    'physical reads',
    'physical reads direct');
```

Some quick things to look for in the above statistics:

- Increasing numbers of physical reads and a low hit ratio *may* indicate insufficient settings for *db_block_buffers* or *db_cache_size* (Oracle9i). The hit ratio reading in particular should be observed over a decent time period to see if the ratio is representative of the database's 'personality', so keep in mind that readings below the normal 'rule of thumb' (90%) can be OK.

- High volumes of disk sorts could be indicative of either a setting for *sort_area_size* (Oracle8i and below) that is too low or unnecessary sort activities. Seeing large numbers of physical writes in a read-only database may also be indicative of excessive sorting.

- Large numbers of user rollbacks can be undesirable, since it indicates that user transactions are not completing for one reason or another.

You should also do a cursory, global check of the system-level wait events to get an idea of the I/O bottlenecks that may be occurring. A script like the *syswaits.sql* script can be used to perform such a check:

syswaits.sql

```
select
   event,
   total_waits,
   round(100 * (total_waits / sum_waits),2) pct_waits,
   time_wait_sec,
   round(100 * (time_wait_sec / greatest(sum_time_waited,1)),2)
   pct_time_waited,
   total_timeouts,
   round(100 * (total_timeouts / greatest(sum_timeouts,1)),2)
   pct_timeouts,
   average_wait_sec
from
(select
```

```
        event,
        total_waits,
        round((time_waited / 100),2) time_wait_sec,
        total_timeouts,
        round((average_wait / 100),2) average_wait_sec
from
        sys.v_$system_event
where
        event not in
('lock element cleanup',
 'pmon timer',
 'rdbms ipc message',
 'rdbms ipc reply',
 'smon timer',
 'SQL*Net message from client',
 'SQL*Net break/reset to client',
 'SQL*Net message to client',
 'SQL*Net more data from client',
 'dispatcher timer',
 'Null event',
 'parallel query dequeue wait',
 'parallel query idle wait - Slaves',
 'pipe get',
 'PL/SQL lock timer',
 'slave wait',
 'virtual circuit status',
 'WMON goes to sleep') and
 event not like 'DFS%' and
 event not like 'KXFX%'),
(select
        sum(total_waits) sum_waits,
        sum(total_timeouts) sum_timeouts,
        sum(round((time_waited / 100),2)) sum_time_waited
   from
        sys.v_$system_event
   where
        event not in
 ('lock element cleanup',
 'pmon timer',
 'rdbms ipc message',
 'rdbms ipc reply',
 'smon timer',
 'SQL*Net message from client',
 'SQL*Net break/reset to client',
 'SQL*Net message to client',
 'SQL*Net more data from client',
 'dispatcher timer',
 'Null event',
 'parallel query dequeue wait',
 'parallel query idle wait - Slaves',
 'pipe get',
 'PL/SQL lock timer',
 'slave wait',
 'virtual circuit status',
 'WMON goes to sleep') and
 event not like 'DFS%' and
 event not like 'KXFX%')
order by
```

```
2 desc, 1 asc;
```

Output from this query could resemble something like this:

	EVENT	TOTAL_WAITS	PCT_WAITS	TIME_WAIT_SEC	PCT_TIME_WAITED	TOTAL_TIMEOUTS	PCT_TIMEOUTS	AVERAGE_WAIT_SEC
1	control file parallel write	13763	66.1	11.8	43.77	0	0	0
2	direct path write	2216	10.64	4.18	15.5	0	0	0
3	db file sequential read	1874	9	1.76	6.53	0	0	0
4	control file sequential read	1805	8.67	3.86	14.32	0	0	0
5	direct path read	319	1.53	1.11	4.12	0	0	0
6	refresh controlfile command	231	1.11	1.7	6.31	0	0	.01
7	log file parallel write	165	.79	.1	.37	0	0	0
8	db file scattered read	130	.62	.11	.41	0	0	0
9	file open	130	.62	.75	2.78	0	0	.01
10	log file sync	51	.24	.5	1.85	0	0	.01
11	db file parallel write	46	.22	.39	1.45	0	0	.01
12	file identify	35	.17	.06	.22	0	0	0
13	latch free	22	.11	.52	1.93	21	100	.02
14	library cache pin	12	.06	0	0	0	0	0
15	buffer busy waits	10	.05	.12	.45	0	0	.01
16	log file sequential read	5	.02	0	0	0	0	0
17	log file single write	5	.02	0	0	0	0	0
18	instance state change	1	0	0	0	0	0	0
19	library cache load lock	1	0	0	0	0	0	0
20	reliable message	1	0	0	0	0	0	0

Figure 6.1 – System event waits output

A few quick things to note about the output from the waits SQL script:

- Numerous waits for the *db file scattered read* event may indicate a problem with table scans

- Many waits for the *latch free* event could indicate excessive amounts of logical I/O activity

- High wait times for the *enqueue* event pinpoints a problem with lock contention

Once you have a feel for the I/O numbers at a global level, you can begin to work your way further down into what is really going on under the covers.

Determine Global Object Access Patterns

Oracle has come a long way in helping the database professional determine how objects in the database are being accessed. Oracle9i, in particular, has introduced some wonderful new statistical views that can be queried to get a handle on object access patterns. If you have not moved up to 9i yet, do not worry, as there are still methods you can use to understand the I/O occurring against your database.

You should begin with a global sweep of access pattern activity. A query such as the *globaccpatt.sql* script can be used for that:

globaccpatt.sql

```
select
    name,
    value
from
    sys.v_$sysstat
where
    name in
    ('table scans (cache partitions)',
     'table scans (direct read)',
     'table scans (long tables)',
     'table scans (rowid ranges)',
     'table scans (short tables)',
     'table fetch by rowid',
     'table fetch continued row')
order by
    1;
```

Results from such a query might look like this:

```
NAME                                VALUE
------------------------------------  ------
table fetch by rowid                146540
table fetch continued row              698
table scans (cache partitions)           0
table scans (direct read)                0
table scans (long tables)                0
table scans (rowid ranges)               0
table scans (short tables)             262
```

When reviewing the output from the above query, focus on these things:

- Long table scans are typically an activity to avoid, as they have the capability to cause needless physical and logical I/O, as well as flood the buffer cache with seldom-referenced blocks of data. We will find out in a subsequent chapter exactly how to find the large tables that are being scanned, and we will show a quick script that will uncover them.

- The *table fetch continued row* statistic is indicative of chained/migrated row I/O. Such activity is not desired because chained/migrated row access can cause twice the I/O needed to access a table. This is because Oracle must do two or more I/O's to read a chained/migrated row in a table. If high numbers in the *table fetch continued row* statistic are present, then you should determine the percentage of such activity in the overall I/O of the database. This can be obtained from the following *chainpct.sql* script:

chainpct.sql

```
select
   round(100 * (chained_row_fetches /
   total_fetches),2) pct_chain_access
from
   (select
      value as chained_row_fetches
   from
      sys.v_$sysstat a
   where
      name = 'table fetch continued row'),
   (select
      sum(value) as total_fetches
   from
      sys.v_$sysstat
   where
      name in ('table fetch by rowid',
               'table scan rows gotten'));
```

Should the query above return anything over 25%, then your database is likely suffering from a bad case of chained/migrated rows (or perhaps a very hot chained/migrated row table is being accessed repeatedly). You can get a quick idea of how many tables in your database suffer from such a condition by issuing the *chaincnt.sql* query:

---
chaincnt.sql

```
select
      count(*)
from
      sys.tab$
where
      chncnt > 0;
```

The actual tables that contain chained rows can be found by using the *chaintables.sql* query:

---
chaintables.sql

```
select
      owner,
      table_name
from
      sys.dba_tables
where
      chain_cnt > 0;
```

Once you get a general feel for the I/O methods that Oracle uses to access the database objects, you can begin to locate the areas of the database that are most affected.

Examine Storage-level Statistics

Understanding where the storage-level hot spots of a database are is beneficial for a couple of reasons:

- You can get a feel for overworked physical disks by viewing I/O statistics at the tablespace and datafile levels. If a particular disk or set of disks is under too much strain, you can either relocate the tablespaces to less-used devices or create new tablespaces on different disks and move hot objects onto them (assuming, of course, you have extra disks available).

- If you have followed standard DBA practice and placed indexes in their own tablespace, you can view the I/O statistics for that tablespace and see if the indexes are actually being used

To get a feel for physical I/O at the tablespace and datafile level, you can use the *fileio7.sql* query if you are using Oracle 7.3.4 through 8.0:

fileio7.sql

```
select
    d.name file_name,
    c.name tablespace_name,
    b.phyrds,
    b.phywrts,
    b.phyblkrd,
    b.phyblkwrt,
    b.readtim,
    b.writetim
from
    sys.v_$datafile a,
    sys.v_$filestat b,
    sys.ts$ c,
    sys.v_$dbfile d,
    sys.file$ e
where
    a.file# = b.file#
and
    a.file# = d.file#
and
    e.ts# = c.ts#
 and
    e.file# = d.file#
 order by
    b.phyrds desc;
```

If you are using Oracle 8i or higher, you will need the *fileio8plus.sql* query, since these versions of Oracle have temp files in addition to regular datafiles:

fileio8plus.sql

```
select
    d.name file_name,
    c.name tablespace_name,
    b.phyrds,
    b.phywrts,
    b.phyblkrd,
    b.phyblkwrt,
    b.readtim,
    b.writetim
from
    sys.v_$datafile a,
    sys.v_$filestat b,
    sys.ts$ c,
    sys.v_$dbfile d,
    sys.file$ e
where
    a.file# = b.file#
and
    a.file# = d.file#
and
    e.ts# = c.ts#
and
    e.file# = d.file#
union all
select
    v.fnnam file_name,
    c.name tablespace_name,
    b.phyrds,
    b.phywrts,
    b.phyblkrd,
    b.phyblkwrt,
    b.readtim,
    b.writetim
from
    sys.v_$tempfile a,
    sys.v_$tempstat b,
    sys.ts$ c,
    sys.x$kccfn v,
    sys.x$ktfthc hc
where
    a.file# = b.file#
and
    a.file# = hc.ktfthctfno
and
    hc.ktfthctsn = c.ts#
and
    v.fntyp = 7
and
    v.fnnam is not null
and
    v.fnfno = hc.ktfthctfno
and
    hc.ktfthctsn = c.ts#
order by
    3 desc;
```

Output from one of the previous queries would look like this:

	FILE_NAME	TABLESPACE_NAME	PHYRDS	PHYWRTS	PHYBLKRD	PHYBLKWRT	READTIM	WRITETIM
1	D:\ORACLE\ORA92\O92\SYSTEM01.DBF	SYSTEM	22735	1318	29987	1318	6581	331
2	D:\ORACLE\ORA92\O92\XDB01.DBF	XDB	2979	2	2990	2	850	5
3	D:\ORACLE\ORA92\O92\OEM_REPOSITORY.DBF	OEM_REPOSITORY	1582	2	1582	2	487	5
4	D:\ORACLE\ORA92\O92\USERS01.DBF	USERS	554	55	619	55	213	20
5	D:\ORACLE\ORA92\O92\DRSYS01.DBF	DRSYS	282	2	282	2	129	3
6	D:\ORACLE\ORA92\O92\TOOLS01.DBF	TOOLS	84	0	84	0	48	0
7	D:\ORACLE\ORA92\O92\UNDOTBS01.DBF	UNDOTBS1	46	8567	46	8567	709	484
8	D:\ORACLE\ORA92\O92\INDX01.DBF	INDX	11	2	11	2	49	5
9	D:\ORACLE\ORA92\O92\AUTOSEG.ORA	AUTOSEG	6	2	6	2	24	2

Figure 6.2 – Datafile and tablespace I/O details

Some areas to consider when viewing the output of these queries:

- A lot of activity in the SYSTEM tablespace and datafiles may indicate a lot of recursive calls (space management, etc.). Space management problems incurred from data dictionary references can be alleviated by implementing locally-managed tablespaces (Oracle8i and higher).

- Temporary tablespaces (devoted to sort activity) showing higher volumes of physical I/O could indicate a problem with excessive disk activity.

- Quickly review all the physical I/O for each drive/file system and get a feel for the overworked disks on your server. If you have underutilized disk drives (with their own controllers), then you should consider relocating some tablespaces that exhibit high I/O characteristics to those drives.

Now that you know how to find tablespace and datafile hotspots, the next step is to determine the actual objects under constant pressure.

Locating Hot I/O Objects

Once you know where the hotspots in your database are with respect to storage structures, it is time to drill further down and locate the objects that are most in demand. There is no doubt that hub tables in a system can cause a major I/O bottleneck if they are not correctly designed and implemented.

To get an idea of which objects have been the "favorite" of a database's SQL calls, you can run the following *toptables.sql* query, which gets the top 100 objects as determined by SQL statement execution:

toptables.sql

```
select
   table_owner "table owner",
   table_name "table name",
   command "command issued",
   0 - executions    "executions",
   disk_reads "disk reads",
   gets "buffer gets",
   rows_processed "rows processed"
from
(select
        distinct executions,
                 command,
                 table_owner,
                 table_name,
                 gets,
                 rows_processed,
                 disk_reads
 from
(select
        decode (a.command_type ,
                2, 'insert ' ,
                3,'select ',
                6, 'update  ' ,
                7, 'delete ' ,
                26,'table lock  ') command ,
                c.owner table_owner,
                c.name table_name ,
                sum(a.disk_reads) disk_reads ,
                sum(0 - a.executions) executions ,
                sum(a.buffer_gets) gets  ,
```

```
                    sum(a.rows_processed) rows_processed
from
        sys.v_$sql   a ,
        sys.v_$object_dependency b ,
        sys.v_$db_object_cache    c
where
        a.command_type in (2,3,6,7,26)and
        b.from_address = a.address and
        b.to_owner = c.owner and
        b.to_name= c.name and
        c.type = 'table' and
        c.owner not in ('SYS','SYSTEM')
group by
        a.command_type , c.owner  , c.name )  )
where
        rownum <= 100;
```

Output from the above query might look like this:

	TABLE OWNER	TABLE NAME	COMMAND ISSUED	EXECUTIONS	DISK READS	BUFFER GETS	ROWS PROCESSED
1	ERADMIN	TESTXML_927	SELECT	13	2	131	0
2	ERADMIN	ADMISSION	SELECT	7	13	184	2508
3	ERADMIN	TESTXML_927NEW2	SELECT	4	0	94	0
4	ERADMIN	TESTLOB_NEW	SELECT	2	5	127	2
5	ERADMIN	ADMISSION_TEST	SELECT	1	1	111	0
6	ERADMIN	MEDICATION_DISP	SELECT	1	1	32	0
7	ERADMIN	PATIENT_PROCEDURE	SELECT	1	5	23	0
8	ERADMIN	TESTXML_927NEW	SELECT	1	0	53	3
9	WMSYS	WM$ENV_VARS	SELECT	1	8	403	1
10	WMSYS	WM$VERSIONED_TABLES	SELECT	1	8	403	1
11	WMSYS	WM$VERSION_HIERARCHY_TABLE	SELECT	1	8	403	1

Figure 6.3 – Top tables query output

Observing a single table with a lot of DML activity provides a clue that it may be a potential bottleneck for your system. Other things to consider when reviewing output from this query include:

- Small, frequently-accessed tables should be considered candidates for the Oracle KEEP buffer pool (Oracle8i and higher) or be set to CACHE (Oracle7 and higher).

- Large tables that are often accessed and scanned should be reviewed to determine if they could be partitioned. Partitioning can reduce scan times if only one or a handful of partitions can be scanned instead of the entire table. High amounts of disk reads for tables in the above query are red flags that can help you identify partitioning possibilities.

If you think that large tables are being scanned, and you are using Oracle9i, you can make use of the new *v_$sql_plan* view to validate your suspicions. The *largescan9i.sql* query uses this new view to show which large tables (defined in the query as tables over 1MB) are being scanned in the database:

---

largescan9i.sql

```
select
    table_owner,
    table_name,
    table_type,
    size_kb,
    statement_count,
    reference_count,
    executions,
    executions * reference_count total_scans
from
    (select
        a.object_owner table_owner,
        a.object_name table_name,
        b.segment_type table_type,
        b.bytes / 1024 size_kb,
        sum(c.executions ) executions,
        count( distinct a.hash_value ) statement_count,
        count( * ) reference_count
    from
        sys.v_$sql_plan a,
        sys.dba_segments b,
        sys.v_$sql c
    where
        a.object_owner (+) = b.owner
    and
            a.object_name (+) = b.segment_name
and
            b.segment_type IN ('TABLE', 'TABLE PARTITION')
and
            a.operation LIKE '%TABLE%'
and
            a.options = 'FULL'
and
            a.hash_value = c.hash_value
and
            b.bytes / 1024 > 1024
group by
    a.object_owner,
```

```
     a.object_name,
     a.operation,
     b.bytes / 1024,
     b.segment_type
order by
     4 desc, 1, 2 );
```

	TABLE_OWNER	TABLE_NAME	TABLE_TYPE	SIZE_KB	STATEMENT_COUNT	REFERENCE_COUNT	EXECUTIONS	TOTAL_SCANS
1	ERADMIN	EMP	TABLE	19456	2	2	2	4
2	SYS	DEPENDENCY$	TABLE	3496	1	1	1	1
3	SYS	OBJ$	TABLE	3136	4	7	25	175

Figure 6.4 – Output from the 9i large table scan query

After finding out *what* is being accessed the most, you next move into finding out *who* is causing all the activity.

Find the Current I/O Session Bandits

If the complaint of poor performance is current, then the connected sessions are one of the first things to check to see which users are impacting the system in undesirable ways. There are a couple of different avenues to take here.

First, you can get an idea of the percentage that each session is/has taken up with respect to I/O. One rule of thumb is that if any session is currently consuming 50% or more of the total I/O, then that session and its SQL need to be investigated further to determine what activity it is engaged in.

If you are a DBA that is just concerned with physical I/O, then the *physpctio.sql* query will provide the information you need:

---
physpctio.sql

```
select
```

```
      sid,
      username,
      round(100 * total_user_io/total_io,2) tot_io_pct
from
(select
      b.sid sid,
      nvl(b.username,p.name) username,
      sum(value) total_user_io
 from
      sys.v_$statname c,
      sys.v_$sesstat a,
      sys.v_$session b,
      sys.v_$bgprocess p
 where
      a.statistic#=c.statistic# and
      p.paddr (+) = b.paddr and
      b.sid=a.sid and
      c.name in ('physical reads',
                 'physical writes',
                 'physical writes direct',
                 'physical reads direct',
                 'physical writes direct (lob)',
                 'physical reads direct (lob)')
group by
      b.sid, nvl(b.username,p.name)),
(select
      sum(value) total_io
 from
      sys.v_$statname c,
      sys.v_$sesstat a
 where
      a.statistic#=c.statistic# and
      c.name in ('physical reads',
                 'physical writes',
                 'physical writes direct',
                 'physical reads direct',
                 'physical writes direct (lob)',
                 'physical reads direct (lob)'))
order by
      3 desc;
```

If you are a DBA that wants to see the total I/O picture (in other words, both logical and physical I/O), then use the *totpctio.sql* query instead:

---

totpctio.sql

```
SELECT
      SID,
      USERNAME,
      ROUND(100 * TOTAL_USER_IO/TOTAL_IO,2) TOT_IO_PCT
FROM
(SELECT
```

```
            b.SID SID,
            nvl(b.USERNAME,p.NAME) USERNAME,
            SUM(VALUE) TOTAL_USER_IO
FROM
        sys.V_$STATNAME c,
        sys.V_$SESSTAT a,
        sys.V_$SESSION b,
        sys.v_$bgprocess p
WHERE
        a.STATISTIC#=c.STATISTIC# and
        p.paddr (+) = b.paddr and
        b.SID=a.SID and
        c.NAME in ('physical reads','physical writes',
                   'consistent changes','consistent gets',
                   'db block gets','db block changes',
                   'physical writes direct',
                   'physical reads direct',
                   'physical writes direct (lob)',
                   'physical reads direct (lob)')
GROUP BY
        b.SID, nvl(b.USERNAME,p.name)),
(select
        sum(value) TOTAL_IO
from
        sys.V_$STATNAME c,
        sys.V_$SESSTAT a
WHERE
        a.STATISTIC#=c.STATISTIC# and
        c.NAME in ('physical reads','physical writes',
                   'consistent changes',
                   'consistent gets','db block gets',
                   'db block changes',
                   'physical writes direct',
                   'physical reads direct',
                   'physical writes direct (lob)',
                   'physical reads direct (lob)'))
ORDER BY
        3 DESC;
```

Regardless of which query you use, the output might
resemble something like the following:

```
SID     USERNAME        TOT_IO_PCT
-------------------------------
9       USR1               71.26
20      SYS                15.76
5       SMON                7.11
2       DBWR                4.28
12      SYS                 1.42
6       RECO                 .12
7       SNP0                 .01
10      SNP3                 .01
11      SNP4                 .01
8       SNP1                 .01
1       PMON                   0
3       ARCH                   0
4       LGWR                   0
```

In the above example, a DBA would be prudent to examine the USR1 session to see what SQL calls they are making. In a subsequent chapter I'll show how to do this in detail, however for now you can see that the above queries are excellent weapons that you can use to quickly pinpoint problem I/O sessions.

If you want more detail with respect to the top I/O session in a database, you can use the rather large *topiousers.sql* query instead to see all the actual I/O numbers:

---

topiousers.sql

```
select
     b.sid sid,
     decode (b.username,null,e.name,b.username)
     user_name,
     d.spid os_id,
     b.machine machine_name,
     to_char(logon_time,'mm/dd/yy hh:mi:ss pm')
     logon_time,
     (sum(decode(c.name,'physical reads',value,0))
     +
     sum(decode(c.name,'physical writes',value,0))
     +
     sum(decode(c.name,
     'physical writes direct',value,0)) +
     sum(decode(c.name,
     'physical writes direct (lob)',value,0)) +
     sum(decode(c.name,
     'physical reads direct (lob)',value,0)) +
     sum(decode(c.name,
     'physical reads direct',value,0)))
     total_physical_io,
     (sum(decode(c.name,'db block gets',value,0))
     +
     sum(decode(c.name,
     'db block changes',value,0))   +
     sum(decode(c.name,'consistent changes',value,0)) +
     sum(decode(c.name,'consistent gets',value,0)) )
     total_logical_io,
     100 - 100 *(round ((sum (decode
     (c.name, 'physical reads', value, 0)) -
     sum (decode (c.name,
     'physical reads direct', value, 0))) /
     (sum (decode (c.name, 'db block gets',
     value, 1)) +
     sum (decode (c.name, 'consistent gets',
```

```
      value, 0))),3)) hit_ratio,
      sum(decode(c.name,'sorts (disk)',value,0))
      disk_sorts,
      sum(decode(c.name,'sorts (memory)',value,0))
      memory_sorts,
      sum(decode(c.name,'sorts (rows)',value,0))
      rows_sorted,
      sum(decode(c.name,'user commits',value,0))
      commits,
      sum(decode(c.name,'user rollbacks',value,0))
      rollbacks,
      sum(decode(c.name,'execute count',value,0))
      executions,
      sum(decode(c.name,'physical reads',value,0))
      physical_reads,
      sum(decode(c.name,'db block gets',value,0))
      db_block_gets,
      sum(decode(c.name,'consistent gets',value,0))
      consistent_gets,
      sum(decode(c.name,'consistent changes',value,0))
      consistent_changes
from
      sys.v_$sesstat a,
      sys.v_$session b,
      sys.v_$statname c,
      sys.v_$process d,
      sys.v_$bgprocess e
where
      a.statistic#=c.statistic#
and
      b.sid=a.sid
and
      d.addr = b.paddr
and
      e.paddr (+) = b.paddr
and
      c.name in
      ('physical reads',
       'physical writes',
       'physical writes direct',
       'physical reads direct',
       'physical writes direct (lob)',
       'physical reads direct (lob)',
       'db block gets',
       'db block changes',
       'consistent changes',
       'consistent gets',
       'sorts (disk)',
       'sorts (memory)',
       'sorts (rows)',
       'user commits',
       'user rollbacks',
       'execute count'
)
group by
      b.sid,
      d.spid,
      decode (b.username,null,e.name,b.username),
            b.machine,
```

```
            to_char(logon_time,'mm/dd/yy hh:mi:ss pm')
order by
   6 desc;
```

Output from the query above could look like the following:

	SID	USER_NAME	OS_ID	MACHINE_NAME	LOGON_TIME	TOTAL_PHYSICAL_IO	TOTAL_LOGICAL_IO	HIT_RATIO	DISK_SORTS	MEMORY_SORTS	ROWS_SORTED	COMMIT
1	2	DBMO	1064	EBT2K11	12/05/02 03:12:10 PM	9982	0	100	0	0	0	
2	12	ORA_MONITOR	2488	EBT2K\EBT2K08	12/12/02 05:28:18 PM	8527	59015775	100	0	289379	126302548	
3	5	SMON	296	EBT2K11	12/05/02 03:12:11 PM	2657	465527	99.4	0	78	175	
4	3	LGWR	980	EBT2K11	12/05/02 03:12:10 PM	34	0	100	0	0	0	
5	6	RECO	1220	EBT2K11	12/05/02 03:12:11 PM	1	1753	99.9	0	8	48	
6	1	PMON	1032	EBT2K11	12/05/02 03:12:09 PM	0	0	100	0	0	0	
7	4	CKPT	1144	EBT2K11	12/05/02 03:12:10 PM	0	0	100	0	0	0	
8	16	SYS	3956	EBT2K\ROBINWS	12/17/02 04:55:29 PM	0	4	100	0	0	0	
9	11	SYS	3096	EBT2K\ROBINWS	12/17/02 05:26:31 PM	0	235	100	0	66	27449	

Figure 6.5 – Sample Top I/O Users detail output

Such a query can provide details about the actual, raw I/O numbers for each connected session. Armed with this information, you can then begin to drill down into each heavy-hitting I/O session to determine what SQL calls they are making and which sets of SQL are the I/O hogs.

While you now know how to troubleshoot I/O from a user standpoint, you should not forget about all the system activity that is caused by Oracle itself. The next section will help you peer into those areas and uncover any I/O issues that reside there.

Miscellaneous I/O Considerations

Before we leave the discussion on I/O hotspots, there are a couple of remaining items to mention in passing:

- Examining background processes
- Monitoring rollback activity

Examining Background Processes

How can you tell if Oracle's DBWR, LGWR, ARCH or other background processes are experiencing I/O bottlenecks? First, you can issue the *bgact.sql* query to get a general handle on DBWR and LGWR activity:

bgact.sql

```
select
   name,
   value
from
   sys.v_$sysstat
where
   (name like '%DBWR%'
or
    name in
       ('dirty buffers inspected',
        'summed dirty queue length',
        'write requests'))
or
       (name like '%redo%')
order by
    1;
```

The output from the above query might look like this:

```
NAME                                 VALUE
-----------------------------------------
DBWR buffers scanned                     0
DBWR checkpoint buffers written        438
DBWR checkpoints                         0
DBWR cross instance writes               0
DBWR free buffers found                  0
DBWR lru scans                           0
DBWR make free requests                  0
DBWR revisited being-written buffer      0
DBWR summed scan depth                   0
DBWR transaction table writes          151
DBWR undo block writes                 154
dirty buffers inspected                  0
redo blocks written                    804
redo buffer allocation retries           0
redo entries                          1297
redo log space requests                  0
redo log space wait time                 0
redo log switch interrupts               0
redo ordering marks                      0
redo size                           329192
redo synch time                         54
```

```
redo synch writes                   116
redo wastage                        69528
redo write time                     79
redo writer latching time           0
redo writes                         237
summed dirty queue length           0
```

Seeing non-zero values for the DBWR summed dirty queue length typically indicates that buffers are being left in the write queue after a write request. This could signal that the DBWR process is falling behind and that more DBWR processes should be added to the system. Non-zero values for the redo log space wait requests and redo log space wait time statistics could indicate a too-low setting for the log buffer.

Archive log I/O problems can usually be viewed in the form of entries in the Oracle alert log (messages indicating waits for the archive log files to complete).

You can get an idea of how many logs your archive process writes per day by issuing a query like the *archhist.sql* script (which shows the number of logs written per day for the last 30 days):

archhist.sql

```
select
   to_char(completion_time,'mm/dd/yy') completion_time,
   count(*)                            log_count
from
   sys.v_$archived_log
where
   sysdate - completion_time < 31
group by
   to_char(completion_time,'mm/dd/yy')
order by
   1 desc;
```

Once you look at the overall I/O picture of Oracle's background processes, you can then begin to move into specific areas like rollback segments.

Monitoring Rollback Activity

Rollback segments can become hotspots for I/O activity, especially on Oracle8i and below, if a lot of DML activity is occurring in the database. Oracle writes data to individual rollback segments to undo changes made to the Oracle database from within a transaction.

Rollbacks are also used to maintain read consistency for multiple users of modified data.

To check the amount of rollback I/O your database is experiencing, you can use the *rolldet.sql* query:

rolldet.sql

```
select
   name,
   round ((rssize / 1024), 2) size_kb,
   shrinks,
   extends,
   gets,
   waits,
   writes,
   xacts,
   status,
   round ((hwmsize / 1024), 2) hw_kb
from
   sys.v_$rollstat a,
   sys.v_$rollname b
where
   (a.usn = b.usn)
order by
   name;
```

Here is a sample of the output:

	NAME	SIZE_KB	SHRINKS	EXTENDS	GETS	WAITS	WRITES	XACTS	STATUS	HW_KB
1	RBS0	4088	0	0	3572	0	3624	0	ONLINE	4088
2	RBS1	4088	0	0	3573	0	6194	0	ONLINE	4088
3	RBS10	4088	0	0	3569	0	8252	0	ONLINE	4088
4	RBS11	4088	0	0	3568	0	1650	0	ONLINE	4088
5	RBS12	4088	0	0	3566	0	1266	0	ONLINE	4088
6	RBS13	4088	0	0	3566	0	1150	0	ONLINE	4088
7	RBS14	4088	0	0	3566	0	1420	0	ONLINE	4088
8	RBS15	4088	0	0	3566	0	1152	0	ONLINE	4088
9	RBS16	4088	0	0	3566	0	1480	0	ONLINE	4088
10	RBS17	4088	0	0	3566	0	4448	0	ONLINE	4088
11	RBS18	4088	0	0	3566	0	1436	0	ONLINE	4088
12	RBS19	4088	0	0	3567	0	4266	0	ONLINE	4088
13	RBS2	4088	0	0	3575	0	3874	0	ONLINE	4088
14	RBS20	4088	0	0	3566	0	994	0	ONLINE	4088
15	RBS21	4088	0	0	3566	0	1054	0	ONLINE	4088
16	RBS22	4088	0	0	3566	0	1044	0	ONLINE	4088
17	RBS23	4088	0	0	3566	0	1214	0	ONLINE	4088
18	RBS24	4088	0	0	3568	0	1556	0	ONLINE	4088
19	RBS25	4088	0	0	3568	0	1528	0	ONLINE	4088

Figure 6.6 – Rollback activity details

To properly tune rollback I/O, you must first make sure that you have enough segments to accommodate the workload of the database. Constantly seeing a count of active rollback segments equal to or near the number of rollbacks defined for the database is an indicator that you should create more.

An overall rollback contention ratio of 1% or higher is an indicator of too few rollbacks, as well. Seeing wait counts greater than zero for each rollback segment is further evidence that you should create more rollback segments. If you are using Oracle9i, then you can make use of the new UNDO tablespace feature that allows Oracle to automatically manage all rollback activity for you, including dynamically allocating more rollback segments when it becomes necessary.

After ensuring that enough rollback segments exist in the database, you should turn your attention to the question of sizing. Dynamic rollback extension can take a toll on performance if you consistently enlarge segments to accommodate heavy transaction loads.

Seeing rollback segments undergoing numerous extends and shrinks (as Oracle returns a segment back to its OPTIMAL setting), as well as rollback segments with current or high watermark sizes greater than their OPTIMAL setting, usually is a good indicator that you should permanently enlarge them.

Conclusion

It is certainly not easy keeping track of all the I/O activity in a heavy-duty database, but by following the roadmap provided in this chapter and using the included scripts, you should be able to quickly uncover all the hotspots in any Oracle database you manage.

By starting with global I/O statistics and moving through I/O at the storage structure, object, and user levels, you can quickly determine where your I/O hotspots are and then start working to make things better.

The next chapter will look at how you can eliminate the major bottlenecks in your system by using both wait-based and extended analytical techniques.

Chapter 7

Workload Analysis Part 1 - Uncovering Problem Sessions

It's an old joke among database administrators that databases would run just fine if no users were allowed to connect to them. Of course this isn't the case, and with the internet-enabled database applications, it's possible to have databases with virtually no limit to the number of users that can connect to the system. Also, as user load increases, there is an increased need to manage the performance of your database with respect to user and code activity.

Your performance strategy should include solid techniques for quickly identifying database sessions that are using excessive resources, or causing system bottlenecks. In an earlier chapter, you learned that you should use ratio-based and bottleneck analysis techniques when troubleshooting Oracle databases.

When you begin examining session and SQL activity, you use a third analytic technique referred to as *workload analysis*. In this chapter, you'll learn how to perform workload analysis by looking at session activity, using a variety of analysis techniques and scripts. The main topics of discussion are:

- Uncovering Security Holes

- Finding Storage Hogs

- Locating Top Resource Sessions

- Pinpointing Sessions with Problem SQL

You begin by looking at security holes, because you only want the user accounts that belong on a system to be the ones that are actually there.

Uncovering Security Holes

As a DBA, you should first ensure that no user account can access any storage or database object that it shouldn't. While identifying such accounts can get tricky, depending on the complexity of the database, there are a few general sweeps you should make from time to time to uncover potential security holes in a system.

First, you should check to see that no general users are granted powerful roles, such as DBA. A query like the *dbagranted.sql* script can determine if such is the case.

---
dbagranted.sql

```
select
    grantee
from
    sys.dba_role_privs
where
    granted_role = 'dba'
and
    grantee not in ('SYS','SYSTEM');
```

Likewise, you check to see if any user accounts have been granted sensitive privileges, or roles that provide them with the potential to cause serious damage to the database. For example, a user with the *unlimited tablespace* privilege can place data in the SYSTEM tablespace, which should only be reserved for data dictionary objects. The *sensprivs.sql* script can help you quickly find such accounts.

---

sensprivs.sql

```
select
   grantee,
   privilege,
   admin_option
from
   sys.dba_sys_privs
where
 (privilege like '%ANY%'
  or
  privilege like '%DROP%'
  or
  privilege in
     ('ALTER SYSTEM',
      'ALTER TABLESPACE',
      'BECOME USER',
      'UNLIMITED TABLESPACE'))
   and
   grantee not in ('SYS','SYSTEM')
   and
   grantee not in
(select role from sys.dba_roles)
union all
select
   grantee,
   privilege,
   admin_option
from
   sys.dba_sys_privs
where
   (privilege like '%ANY%'
   or
    privilege like '%DROP%'
   or
    privilege in
    ('ALTER SYSTEM',
     'ALTER TABLESPACE',
     'BECOME USER',
     'UNLIMITED TABLESPACE'))
   and
     grantee not in ('SYS','SYSTEM')
   and
   grantee in
    (select role
     from sys.dba_roles
     where role not in
     ('DBA',
      'AQ_ADMINISTRATOR_ROLE',
      'IMP_FULL_DATABASE',
      'SNMPAGENT',
      'OEM_MONITOR',
      'EXP_FULL_DATABASE'));
```

If any users do indeed have sensitive privileges or roles, output from the query above might look like this:

```
GRANTEE      PRIVILEGE                ADMIN_OPTION
------------------------------------------------------
BAD_GUY      ALTER ANY PROCEDURE          NO
BAD_GUY      ALTER ANY TRIGGER            NO
BAD_GUY      CREATE ANY INDEX             NO
BAD_GUY      CREATE ANY PROCEDURE         NO
BAD_GUY      CREATE ANY TABLE             NO
BAD_GUY      CREATE ANY TRIGGER           NO
BAD_GUY      DROP ANY PROCEDURE           NO
BAD_GUY      DROP ANY TRIGGER             NO
BAD_GUY      EXECUTE ANY PROCEDURE        NO
BAD_GUY      UNLIMITED TABLESPACE         NO
```

Users found with these two queries should be examined to see if they really need the special privileges that they have been granted. In addition to users having sensitive privileges or roles, you should check to see if any user accounts have undesired abilities with respect to storage.

User accounts with unchecked storage powers can cause major headaches for you as a DBA. The *badstorage.sql* script can be used to find such accounts.

---

badstorage.sql

```
select
     a.name username,'system as default' privilege
from
     sys.user$ a,
     sys.ts$ dts,
     sys.ts$ tts
where
     (a.datats# = dts.ts# and a.tempts# = tts.ts#) and
     (dts.name = 'SYSTEM' or tts.name = 'SYSTEM') and
     a.name not in ('SYS', 'SYSTEM')
union
select
     username,'system quotas'
from
     sys.dba_ts_quotas
where
     tablespace_name = 'system' and
     username not in ('SYS', 'SYSTEM')
union
select
```

```
        grantee,'unlimited tablespace'
from
        dba_sys_privs
where
        privilege = 'unlimited tablespace' and
        grantee not in ('SYS', 'SYSTEM')
order by
        1;
```

If you have user accounts with unchecked storage
capabilities, the output form the query above might look
like this:

```
USERNAME                          PRIVILEGE
------------------------------------------------------
AQ_ADMINISTRATOR_ROLE      SYSTEM AS DEFAULT
BAD_GUY                    UNLIMITED TABLESPACE
BAD_ROLE                   SYSTEM AS DEFAULT
BILLY                      UNLIMITED TABLESPACE
BRKADMIN                   UNLIMITED TABLESPACE
CODER                      UNLIMITED TABLESPACE
```

Any user account that's identified in the *badstorage* query
should be altered, so their storage settings don't have the
potential to impact the database in a negative manner.

Finally, although it's surprising that DBAs in today's very
security-conscious environment would allow this to occur,
you ought to make sure that no critical database exists with
default passwords for the SYS and SYSTEM accounts.

Once you've plugged any database security holes, you
should move on to examining each session's storage
capabilities.

Finding Storage Hogs

One thing you should keep an eye on in your database is
the amount of storage space that each user account is
consuming. It's not uncommon for developers to create

object backups of their object backups when working on a critical project, and if those objects are left indefinitely in the database, you will find yourself with a lot of unusable space that may be needed at a later time.

A good query to run to see how much space each user account has consumed is the *totuserspace.sql* script:

totuserspace.sql

```
select
        owner,
        round((byte_count / 1024 / 1024),2) space_used_mb,
        round(100 * (byte_count / tot_bytes),2) pct_of_database
from
(select
        owner ,
        sum(bytes) as byte_count
from
        sys.dba_segments
where
        segment_type not in ('TEMPORARY','CACHE')
group by
        owner
order by
        2 desc),
(select
        sum(bytes) as tot_bytes
from
        sys.dba_segments);
```

Partial output from the above query might look something like this:

```
OWNER           SPACE_USED_MB        PCT_OF_DATABASE
---------------------------------------------------
ERADMIN           807.10               58.48
SYS               322.36               23.36
USER1              45.47                3.29
REPO               27.19                1.97
SYSTEM             22.88                1.66
```

You should run the above script and examine the output periodically to see if any user accounts are hogging the majority of space in a database. Of course, some databases only have one schema account that contains application objects, so in that case you shouldn't have anything to worry about.

If, however, you notice a number of accounts with large amounts of data, you should check each user to ensure that bogus objects have not been left that both clutter up your user database files, and add to the size of the Oracle data dictionary.

Another storage issue to examine from time to time is the amount of temporary space connected sessions are using. Many DBAs have experienced the sad fact that large disk sorts can cause out of space conditions to manifest quickly, at both the database and operating system level.

To get an idea of historical temporary tablespace (sort) usage, you can execute the *sortusage.sql* query:

---

sortusage.sql

```
select
        tablespace_name,
        current_users,
        total_extents,
        used_extents,
        free_extents,
        max_used_size,
        max_sort_size
from
        sys.v_$sort_segment
order by 1;
```

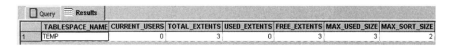

	TABLESPACE_NAME	CURRENT_USERS	TOTAL_EXTENTS	USED_EXTENTS	FREE_EXTENTS	MAX_USED_SIZE	MAX_SORT_SIZE
1	TEMP	0	3	0	3	3	2

Figure 7.1 – Output from the sortusage.sql query

The output will tell you how many users are currently using space in each temporary tablespace, along with the current used extent and free extent numbers. The last two columns will tell you the largest number of total extents ever used for all sorts, and the size of the single largest sort (in extents) since the database has been up.

Such knowledge can help you plan the size of your temporary tablespace(s). Many DBAs will size their temporary tablespaces very large in anticipation of heavy sort activity, only to find that such sorts do not occur. If you don't see heavy temporary tablespace usage, you may be able to resize your temporary tablespace datafiles and reclaim space on your server.

If the *sortusage* query shows that users are currently using space in a temporary tablespace, you may want to dig deeper and see exactly what they're doing. The *sortdet.sql* query can give you this exact detail.

sortdet.sql

```
select
        sql_text,
        sid,
        c.username,
        machine,
        tablespace,
        extents,
        blocks
from
        sys.v_$sort_usage a,
        sys.v_$sqlarea b,
        sys.v_$session c
where
        a.sqladdr = b.address and
        a.sqlhash = b.hash_value and
        a.session_addr = c.saddr
order by
        sid;
```

Output from the above query might look like this:

```
SQL_TEXT        SID   USERNAME  MACHINE TABLESPACE EXTENTS   BLOCKS
-----------------------------------------------------------------
SELECT * FROM   10    ERADMIN   ROBS    TEMP        10        80
```

Using this query, you can get the SQL call, current session information, and details on how much temporary space the SQL call is using. Red flags should begin to run up the flagpole if continuous large disk sorts are occurring on your system.

Sort activity that occurs on disk is much slower than sorts that occur in memory, so you should begin to examine your memory settings, as well as the SQL statements that are uncovered from this query, to see if unnecessary sorts are occurring or if the *init.ora/spfile* parameters relating to sorting are set too low.

Locating Top Resource Sessions

When your phone starts ringing with complaints of performance slowdowns, one of the first things you should do is perform a cursory examination of the workload that exists on the database. You do this by checking:

- What sessions are connected to the database

- What and how much resources each session is using

- What the resource-heavy sessions are/have been executing

There are a number of database monitors on the market that give a 'Top Sessions' view of things. But even if you don't have a third-party monitor at your disposal, you can quickly pinpoint all the various metrics you'll need with just a few queries.

To get a bird's eye view of the top resource users with respect to physical I/O, logical I/O, memory, and CPU, you can execute the rather large *topsess.sql* query on Oracle8i and above.

topsess.sql

```
select
        'top physical i/o process' category,
        sid,
        username,
        total_user_io amt_used,
        round(100 * total_user_io/total_io,2) pct_used
from
(select
         b.sid sid,
         nvl(b.username,p.name) username,
         sum(value) total_user_io
from
     sys.v_$statname c,
     sys.v_$sesstat a,
     sys.v_$session b,
     sys.v_$bgprocess p
where
     a.statistic#=c.statistic# and
     p.paddr (+) = b.paddr and
     b.sid=a.sid and
     c.name in ('physical reads','physical writes',
                'physical reads direct',
                'physical reads direct (lob)',
                'physical writes direct',
                'physical writes direct (lob)')
group by
     b.sid, nvl(b.username,p.name)
order by
     3 desc),
(select
        sum(value) total_io
from
     sys.v_$statname c,
     sys.v_$sesstat a
where
     a.statistic#=c.statistic# and
     c.name in ('physical reads','physical writes',
                'physical reads direct',
                'physical reads direct (lob)',
                'physical writes direct',
```

```
                    'physical writes direct (lob)'))
where
        rownum < 2
union all
select
        'top logical i/o process',
        sid,
        username,
        total_user_io amt_used,
        round(100 * total_user_io/total_io,2) pct_used
from
(select
        b.sid sid,
        nvl(b.username,p.name) username,
        sum(value) total_user_io
from
      sys.v_$statname c,
      sys.v_$sesstat a,
      sys.v_$session b,
      sys.v_$bgprocess p
where
      a.statistic#=c.statistic# and
      p.paddr (+) = b.paddr and
      b.sid=a.sid and
      c.name in ('consistent gets','db block gets')
group by
      b.sid, nvl(b.username,p.name)
order by
      3 desc),
(select
      sum(value) total_io
from
      sys.v_$statname c,
      sys.v_$sesstat a
where
      a.statistic#=c.statistic# and
      c.name in ('consistent gets','db block gets'))
where
      rownum < 2
union all
select
      'top memory process',
      sid,
      username,
      total_user_mem,
      round(100 * total_user_mem/total_mem,2)
from
(select
        b.sid sid,
        nvl(b.username,p.name) username,
        sum(value) total_user_mem
from
        sys.v_$statname c,
        sys.v_$sesstat a,
        sys.v_$session b,
        sys.v_$bgprocess p
where
      a.statistic#=c.statistic# and
```

```
         p.paddr (+) = b.paddr and
         b.sid=a.sid and
         c.name in ('session pga memory','session uga memory')
group by
         b.sid, nvl(b.username,p.name)
order by
         3 desc),
(select
         sum(value) total_mem
from
       sys.v_$statname c,
       sys.v_$sesstat a
where
       a.statistic#=c.statistic# and
       c.name in ('session pga memory','session uga memory') )
where
       rownum < 2
union all
select
         'top cpu process',
         sid,
         username,
         total_user_cpu,
         round(100 * total_user_cpu/greatest(total_cpu,1),2)
from
(select
         b.sid sid,
         nvl(b.username,p.name) username,
         sum(value) total_user_cpu
from
         sys.v_$statname c,
         sys.v_$sesstat a,
         sys.v_$session b,
         sys.v_$bgprocess p
where
         a.statistic#=c.statistic# and
         p.paddr (+) = b.paddr and
         b.sid=a.sid and
         c.name = 'CPU used by this session'
group by
         b.sid, nvl(b.username,p.name)
order by
         3 desc),
(select
         sum(value) total_cpu
from
         sys.v_$statname c,
         sys.v_$sesstat a
where
         a.statistic#=c.statistic# and
         c.name = 'CPU used by this session'  )
where
         rownum < 2;
```

Output from this query might look like this:

```
CATEGORY                    SID        USERNAME  AMT_USED   PCT_USED
-------------------------------------------------------------------
Top Physical I/O Process    19         ORA_USR1  120423120  99.68
Top Logical I/O Process      5         SMON        2774880  25.50
Top Memory Process          19         ORA_USR1    6198492  27.83
Top CPU Process             19         ORA_USR1   15435557  99.75
```

In the above example, a DBA should focus on SID 19, as it seems to have a stranglehold on the system in terms of overall resource consumption. A rule of thumb is that no session should consume more than 25-50% of the overall resources in a particular category. If such is not the case, you should examine each session in more detail to gain insight into what each might be doing.

To drill down and get more detail on across-the-board resource consumption, you might run a query such as the *topsessdet.sql* script.

---

topsessdet.sql

```
select *
        from
(select
        b.sid sid,
        decode (b.username,null,e.name,b.username) user_name,
        d.spid os_id,
        b.machine machine_name,
        to_char(logon_time,'mm/dd/yy hh:mi:ss pm') logon_time,
        (sum(decode(c.name,'physical reads',value,0)) +
        sum(decode(c.name,'physical writes',value,0)) +
        sum(decode(c.name,'physical writes direct',value,0)) +
        sum(decode(c.name,'physical writes direct (lob)',value,0))
        +
        sum(decode(c.name,'physical reads direct (lob)',value,0))
        +
        sum(decode(c.name,'physical reads direct',value,0)))
        total_physical_io,
        (sum(decode(c.name,'db block gets',value,0))  +
        sum(decode(c.name,'db block changes',value,0))  +
        sum(decode(c.name,'consistent changes',value,0)) +
        sum(decode(c.name,'consistent gets',value,0)) )
        total_logical_io,
        100 -
        100 *
        (round ((sum (decode (c.name, 'physical reads', value,
```

```
          0)) -
          sum (decode (c.name, 'physical reads direct', value,
          0))) /
          (sum (decode (c.name, 'db block gets', value, 1)) +
          sum (decode (c.name, 'consistent gets', value, 0))
          ),3)) hit_ratio,
          (sum(decode(c.name,'session pga memory',value,0))+
          sum(decode(c.name,'session uga memory',value,0)) )
          total_memory_usage,
          sum(decode(c.name,'parse count (total)',value,0)) parses,
          sum(decode(c.name,'CPU used by this session',value,0))
          total_cpu,
          sum(decode(c.name,'parse time cpu',value,0)) parse_cpu,
          sum(decode(c.name,'recursive cpu usage',value,0))
          recursive_cpu,
          sum(decode(c.name,'CPU used by this session',value,0)) -
          sum(decode(c.name,'parse time cpu',value,0)) -
          sum(decode(c.name,'recursive cpu usage',value,0))
          other_cpu,
          sum(decode(c.name,'sorts (disk)',value,0)) disk_sorts,
          sum(decode(c.name,'sorts (memory)',value,0)) memory_sorts,
          sum(decode(c.name,'sorts (rows)',value,0)) rows_sorted,
          sum(decode(c.name,'user commits',value,0)) commits,
          sum(decode(c.name,'user rollbacks',value,0)) rollbacks,
          sum(decode(c.name,'execute count',value,0)) executions,
          sum(decode(c.name,'physical reads',value,0))
          physical_reads,
          sum(decode(c.name,'db block gets',value,0)) db_block_gets,
          sum(decode(c.name,'consistent gets',value,0))
          consistent_gets,
          sum(decode(c.name,'consistent changes',value,0))
          consistent_changes
from
          sys.v_$sesstat a,
          sys.v_$session b,
          sys.v_$statname c,
          sys.v_$process d,
          sys.v_$bgprocess e
where
          a.statistic#=c.statistic# and
          b.sid=a.sid   and
          d.addr = b.paddr and
          e.paddr (+) = b.paddr   and
          c.name in ('physical reads',
                  'physical writes',
                  'physical writes direct',
                  'physical reads direct',
                  'physical writes direct (lob)',
                  'physical reads direct (lob)',
                  'db block gets',
                  'db block changes',
                  'consistent changes',
                  'consistent gets',
                  'session pga memory',
                  'session uga memory',
                  'parse count (total)',
                  'CPU used by this session',
                  'parse time cpu',
                  'recursive cpu usage',
```

```
                  'sorts (disk)',
                  'sorts (memory)',
                  'sorts (rows)',
                  'user commits',
                  'user rollbacks',
                  'execute count'
)
group by
        b.sid,
        d.spid,
        decode (b.username,null,e.name,b.username),
        b.machine,
        to_char(logon_time,'mm/dd/yy hh:mi:ss pm')
order by
        6 desc);
```

	SID	USER_NAME	OS_ID	MACHINE_NAME	LOGON_TIME	TOTAL_PHYSICAL_IO	TOTAL_LOGICAL_IO	HIT_RATIO	TOTAL_MEMORY_USAGE	PARSES	TOTAL_CPU	PARSE
1	13	USR1	344	EBT2K\EBT2K08	12/17/02 11:12:45 PM	7209	26147999	100	1646676	39406	52671	
2	2	DBW0	1484	EBT2K04	12/17/02 11:10:30 PM	762	0	100	758700	0	0	
3	5	SMON	2316	EBT2K04	12/17/02 11:10:31 PM	731	38035	98.1	282028	437	0	
4	18	SYS	2512	EBT2K\ROBINWS	12/18/02 01:44:59 PM	343	32345	100	541740	48	112	
5	3	LGWR	2492	EBT2K04	12/17/02 11:10:30 PM	66	0	100	302300	0	0	
6	4	CKPT	2580	EBT2K04	12/17/02 11:10:30 PM	64	0	100	358424	0	0	
7	15	DBSNMP	2304	EBT2K\EBT2K04	12/17/02 11:10:57 PM	37	349	89.9	192968	53	0	
8	12	SYS	2240	EBT2K\ROBINWS	12/18/02 04:26:29 PM	19	101	99.2	434232	20	5	
9	6	RECO	2404	EBT2K04	12/17/02 11:10:31 PM	1	162	99.5	154576	41	0	
10	1	PMON	2628	EBT2K04	12/17/02 11:10:29 PM	0	0	100	78220	0	0	
11	7	SNP0	2416	[NULL]	12/18/02 04:26:17 PM	0	0	100	367832	0	20	
12	8	SNP1	2040	[NULL]	12/18/02 04:26:18 PM	0	0	100	361780	0	14	
13	9	SNP2	2368	[NULL]	12/18/02 04:26:16 PM	0	0	100	214108	0	19	
14	10	SNP3	1668	[NULL]	12/18/02 04:26:17 PM	0	0	100	138300	0	6	
15	11	SNP4	2500	[NULL]	12/18/02 04:26:18 PM	0	0	100	138300	0	6	

Figure 7.2 – Partial top sessions detail output

The output from this query is pretty large, but you can see from the selected columns that you will get a lot more detail from this query than the top session's summary query. For example, the CPU usage is broken down by parse, recursive, and other CPU usage.

Such details will help you determine the exact nature of the work each session has been doing. Once you have located your top sessions, the next step is to locate the SQL calls they've made and determine what 'killer' queries each session has submitted. It may be a case of untuned SQL or inappropriately submitted SQL (such as SQL used for a report that should be run during off hours).

The above queries and scripts are the 'traditional' way of locating problem sessions in your database. However, there are some new techniques you can use to uncover user sessions that might be contributing to an overall decrease in database performance. For example, many DBAs prefer to avoid the continuous scanning of large tables because of the heavy logical and physical I/O cost.

You can locate the currently connected sessions causing such scans in a couple of different ways. The *userscans.sql* query can be used on Oracle to pick out the worst large table scan offenders.

userscans.sql

```
select
        sid,
        username,
        total_user_scans,
        round(100 * total_user_scans/total_scans,2) pct_scans
from
(select
        b.sid sid,
        nvl(b.username,p.name) username,
        sum(value) total_user_scans
from
     sys.v_$statname c,
     sys.v_$sesstat a,
     sys.v_$session b,
     sys.v_$bgprocess p
where
        a.statistic#=c.statistic# and
        p.paddr (+) = b.paddr and
        b.sid=a.sid and
        c.name = 'table scans (long tables)'
group by
        b.sid,
        nvl(b.username,p.name)
order by
        3 desc),
(select
        sum(value) total_scans
from
     sys.v_$statname c,
     sys.v_$sesstat a
where
        a.statistic#=c.statistic# and
```

```
        c.name = 'table scans (long tables)');
```

Sample output from this query might look like this:

```
SID     USERNAME   TOTAL_USER_SCANS   PCT_SCANS
-----------------------------------------------
19      ORA_USER1   2286724             99.94
5       SMON           1397              .06
21      ERADMIN          47             0
1       PMON              0             0
```

Needless to say, if you received output like that shown above, you wouldn't have too much trouble identifying which SID had some explaining to do. Keep in mind that as a DBA, you should normally focus on large table scans vs. small table scans. Often, Oracle can actually digest a small table much easier if it scans it, rather than if it uses an index.

Another way of getting a handle on sessions that are causing table scans is to look at wait events. The *db file scattered read* wait event is generally thought to be an indicator of table scan activity.

The *scatwait.sql* query will yield historical information regarding sessions that have caused *db file scattered read* wait events since the database has been up:

---

scatwait.sql

```
select
       b.sid,
       nvl(b.username,c.name) username,
       b.machine,
       a.total_waits,
       round((a.time_waited / 100),2)
       time_wait_sec,a.total_timeouts,
       round((average_wait / 100),2)
       average_wait_sec,
       round((a.max_wait / 100),2) max_wait_sec
   from
       sys.v_$session_event a,
```

```
        sys.v_$session b,
        sys.v_$bgprocess c
where
        event = 'db file scattered read'
        and a.sid = b.sid
        and c.paddr (+) = b.paddr
order by
        3 desc,
        1 asc;
```

Again, it's not hard to find who the table scan glutton is on this system:

	SID	USERNAME	MACHINE	TOTAL_WAITS	TIME_WAIT_SEC	TOTAL_TIMEOUTS	AVERAGE_WAIT_SEC	MAX_WAIT_SEC
1	13	USR1	EBT2K\EBT2K08	16	.04	0	0	.01
2	5	SMON	EBT2K04	93	0	0	0	0

Figure 7.3 – Detailed wait output for sessions with possible table scans

Note that the drawback of using the above query is that you cannot accurately determine if the waits have been caused by small or large table scans.

While the above queries will work well on Oracle8i and above, you can utilize some new V$ views if you are using Oracle9i. They give you more flexibility identifying problem table scan situations.

The *9ilarge_scanusers.sql* query can help you ferret out the parsing users submitting SQL calls that have scanned tables over 1MB.

9ilarge_scanusers.sql

```
select
        c.username username,
        count(a.hash_value) scan_count
from
        sys.v_$sql_plan a,
        sys.dba_segments b,
        sys.dba_users c,
        sys.v_$sql d
where
        a.object_owner (+) = b.owner
```

```
and    a.object_name (+) = b.segment_name
and    b.segment_type in ('TABLE', 'TABLE PARTITIOn')
and    a.operation like '%TABLE%'
and    a.options = 'FULL'
and    c.user_id = d.parsing_user_id
and    d.hash_value = a.hash_value
and    b.bytes / 1024 > 1024
group by
    c.username
order by
    2 desc;
```

Output from such a query might look like this:

```
USERNAME          SCAN_COUNT
----------     ----------------
SYSTEM                    15
SYS                       13
ORA_USR1                   2
```

You can tweak the above query to locate scans on larger tables by changing the "and b.bytes / 1024 > 1024" clause. Large table scans identified in the *v$sessstat* view are generally thought to be scans that were performed on a table of five blocks or greater.

The above query allows you the flexibility to define 'large' in your own terms. However, regardless of what query you use, if you find sessions that appear to be causing a lot of table scans, the next step is to capture the SQL calls those sessions are issuing, and begin the SQL examination/tuning process.

One final area to examine with respect to problem sessions that are using/holding resources is blocking locks. If the phone calls you receive about performance are complaining about complete gridlock, you can bet that a blocking lock situation exists. If you suspect that's the case, you can issue a few queries that should get right to the heart of the matter.

To get an idea if any blocking locks exist on your database, you can submit the *lockcnt.sql* query.

lockcnt.sql

```
select
       count(*)
from
       sys.v_$session
where
       lockwait is not null;
```

Any non-zero number indicates a current blocking lock situation and can be investigated further by running this query:

```
select
       a.username blocked_user,
       b.username blocking_user,
       w.sid waiting_session,
       h.sid holding_session,
       w.type,
       decode(h.lmode, 1,'no lock',
                       2,'row share',
                       3,'row exclusive',
                   4,'share',
                   5,'share row exclusive',
                   6,'exclusive','none') lmode,
       decode(w.request, 1,'no lock',
                   2,'row share',
                   3,'row exclusive',
                   4,'share',
                   5,'share row exclusive',
                   6,'exclusive','none') request,
       a.row_wait_row# row_waited_on,
       w.id1,
       w.id2,
       w.ctime blocked_user_wait_secs,
       u1.name || '.' || t1.name locked_object
from
       sys.v_$lock w,
       sys.v_$lock h,
       sys.v_$session a,
       sys.v_$session b,
       sys.v_$locked_object o,
       sys.user$ u1,
       sys.obj$ t1
where
       h.lmode != 0 and
       w.request != 0 and
       w.type = h.type and
       w.id1 = h.id1 and
```

```
      w.id2 = h.id2 and
      b.sid = h.sid and
      a.sid = w.sid and
      h.sid = o.session_id and
      o.object_id = t1.obj# and
      u1.user# = t1.owner#
order by
      4,3;
```

Pinpointing Sessions with Problem SQL

Although this section mentions finding problem SQL (and the sessions that are making the problem SQL calls), the bulk of the discussion about finding the most resource intensive SQL code that has run on a database will be saved for the next chapter. The focus here is to pinpoint the problem sessions that are currently issuing bad SQL calls, rather than create a historical analysis of the worst SQL issued on a system.

For example, let's say you would like to see the SQL currently running in a database session that has caused the most physical I/O. A query like the *curriosql.sql* script would do the trick for Oracle8i and above.

---

curriosql.sql

```
select
        sid,
        username,
        sql_text
from
      sys.v_$sqltext a,
      sys.v_$session b
where
      b.sql_address = a.address
      and b.sid =
(select
      sid
from
(select
        b.sid sid,
        nvl(b.username,p.name) username,
        sum(value) total_user_io
from
```

```
     sys.v_$statname c,
     sys.v_$sesstat a,
     sys.v_$session b,
     sys.v_$bgprocess p
where
     a.statistic#=c.statistic# and
     p.paddr (+) = b.paddr and
     b.sid=a.sid and
     c.name in ('physical reads','physical writes',
                'physical reads direct',
                'physical reads direct (lob)',
                'physical writes direct',
                'physical writes direct (lob)')
group by
     b.sid,
     nvl(b.username,p.name)
order by
     3 desc)
where
     rownum < 2)
order by
     a.piece;
```

Output from such a query might look like this:

```
SID    USERNAME      SQL_TEXT
-------------------------------------------------------
19     ORA_MONITOR   SELECT COUNT(*) FROM ADMISSION
19     ORA_MONITOR   WHERE PATIENT_ID BETWEEN 1 AND 100;
```

You could issue similar queries to uncover the SQL that the current memory or CPU is running as well. Of course, the above query will give you only the currently running SQL for a session, which may or may not be the code that has contributed to the session's resource consumption.

If you're running Oracle9i or above, you can do some higher-level analysis to answer questions like "What sessions have parsed Cartesian join statements", by issuing the *cartsession.sql* script.

---

cartsession.sql

```
select
     username,
     count(distinct c.hash_value) nbr_stmts
from
     sys.v_$sql a,
```

```
      sys.dba_users b,
      sys.v_$sql_plan c
where
      a.parsing_user_id = b.user_id
      and    options = 'cartesian'
      and    operation like '%join%'
      and    a.hash_value = c.hash_value
group by
      username
order by
      2 desc;
```

Running this query on an Oracle9i server may yield results similar to this:

```
USERNAME        NBR_STMTS
---------       ---------
ORA_USR1                2
SYSMAN                  2
ERADMIN                 1
```

Once you determine that Cartesian joins have occurred on a system, you can look further and find the actual SQL statements themselves by using a query like the *cartsql.sql* script (again, only on Oracle9i or above).

cartsql.sql

```
select
      *
from
      sys.v_$sql
where
      hash_value in
(select
      hash_value
from
      sys.v_$sql_plan
where
      options = 'CARTESIAN'
      and operation LIKE '%JOIN%' )
order by
      hash_value;
```

	SQL_TEXT	SHARABLE_MEM	PERSISTENT_MEM	RUNTIME_MEM	SORTS	LOADED_VERSIONS	OPEN_VERSIONS	USERS_OPENING
1	SELECT bc_hit_ratio, lib_cache_hit_ratio, dd_cache_hit_ratio, mem_sort_ratio, parse_execute_ratio, buffer_busy_wait_ratio, rollback_cont_ratio, latch_miss_ratio, parallel_query_busy_ratio, percent_shared_pool_free, problem_tablespaces, problem_objects,	834152	14836	135372	37	1	0	0
2	SELECT round((total_space_perm + total_space_temp) - (total_free_space_perm + nvl(total_free_space_temp,0)))/1048576,2) total_used_space, ROUND((total_free_space_perm +	110462	3276	31412	0	1	0	0
3	Select owner, object_type, ' ' Result_Type, object_name from DBA_OBJECTS Where ((object_name like :oLike) or (object_name like :lnName)) and (owner= owner) UNION Select allo.owner, Decode(allo.object_type,'VIEW', 'VIEW COLUMN', 'TABLE', 'TABLE COLUMN'), atc.table_name Result_Type, atc.column_name object_name from	448563	11796	226760	6	1	0	0
4	select username, 1 from DBA_USERS where username='SYS' union select role,2 from DBA_ROLES where role='DBA' union select name, 3 from	101560	3496	60056	3	1	0	0
5	SELECT 900, (total_space - total_free_space)/1048576 FROM (SELECT SUM(bytes) AS total_space FROM	79076	2388	22848	0	1	1	1
6	SELECT bc_hit_ratio, lib_cache_hit_ratio, dd_cache_hit_ratio, mem_sort_ratio, parse_execute_ratio, buffer_busy_wait_ratio, rollback_cont_ratio, latch_miss_ratio, parallel_query_busy_ratio, percent_shared_pool_free, problem_tablespaces, problem_objects,	835631	14836	135372	37	1	0	0
7	SELECT ((total_space_perm + total_space_temp) - (total_free_space_perm +	110811	3216	31176	0	1	0	0

Figure 7.4 – SQL statements that contain at least one Cartesian join

The above script is quite valuable as Cartesian joins can cause unnecessary system workload and be difficult to spot in SQL queries with many join predicates.

Conclusion

While there's no way you can totally prevent users from accessing your database in ways you don't want, you can limit their resource privileges, uncover problem access patterns, and find excessive usage by applying the techniques and scripts highlighted in this chapter. When doing so, you will be applying the starting techniques of another very valuable form of performance analysis, termed workload analysis.

Once you know what the problem sessions are, you can then turn your attention to finding, and either removing or tuning the problem SQL calls that are causing any system slowdowns. This second set of workload analysis techniques will be covered in the next chapter.

Chapter 8

Workload Analysis Part 2 - Identifying Problem SQL

An all time favorite SQL story actually happened on a Teradata system and not Oracle, but it still demonstrates how important it is to find bad SQL, preferably before it's let loose on an unsuspecting database. "Bob" was a really nice guy, but an absolute novice at writing SQL code. Bob was fresh out of computer science school and was hired at a large national insurance company.

The company maintained insurance claim information dating back to approximately the time of Noah's flood, so you can imagine the volume of data that was managed. Because of this, the company purchased a very expensive and large Teradata system that served as the company's data warehouse. Bob was placed into a group of SQL developers that were charged with the task of writing decision support queries against the mammoth Teradata warehouse.

One day Bob asked the DBA group to look at a query he had written against the warehouse, which really was an absolute monster. If you've never had the pleasure of working with Teradata, then you have missed a treat because it is a true database junkie's dream come true. Infinitely scalable architecture, massive parallel processors, tons of RAM, and fast hashing algorithms are used to distribute the tons of data among its many storage devices.

Teradata also has a unique EXPLAIN plan that not only communicates the paths used to obtain a SQL result set, but also gives a time estimate of how long it believes the query will take to run.

Bob was asked if he had run his query through the EXPLAIN utility and he said that he had not, and in fact didn't know that such a thing existed. So without reviewing his query, it was put through an EXPLAIN. Teradata went through its computations and issued back a response. The year that this happened was 1993 and according to Teradata, Bob's query (if executed) would not finish *until the year 2049.*

This story is completely true and highlights how damaging SQL can be in untrained hands. And unfortunately, there are a lot of SQL novices out in IT shops right now getting ready to submit "the big one", and their number is growing. Faced with a shortage of qualified database personnel, companies are throwing guys like Bob into the meat grinder and are expecting them to write SQL code that meets the response time expectations of end users.

As a DBA, you need to have the right game plan in place for finding and fixing problem SQL code in your database. Fortunately, Oracle is better than most DBMSs at providing information in the data dictionary to help a DBA locate and analyze potentially bad SQL. By using the roadmap and scripts provided in this chapter, you should be able make short work of pinpointing any bad SQL that's run though your system.

What is 'Bad SQL'?

Before you can identify problem SQL in your database, you have to ask the question of what 'bad SQL' is. What criteria do you use when you begin the hunt for problem SQL in your critical systems?

Understand that even the seasoned experts disagree on what constitutes efficient and inefficient SQL; so there's no way to sufficiently answer this question to every Oracle professional's satisfaction. What follows are some general criteria you can use when evaluating the output from various database monitors or personal diagnostic scripts:

- **Overall Response (Elapsed) Time** – This is how much time the query took to parse, execute, and fetch the data needed to satisfy the query. It should not include the network time needed to make the round trip from the requesting client workstation to the database server.

- **CPU Time** – This is how much CPU time the query took to parse, execute, and fetch the data needed to satisfy the query.

- **Physical I/O** – Often used as the major statistic in terms of identifying good vs. bad SQL, this is a measure of how many disk reads the query caused to satisfy the user's request. While you certainly want to control disk I/O where possible, it's important that you not focus solely on physical I/O as the single benchmark of inefficient SQL. Make no mistake, disk access is slower than memory access and also consumes processing time making the physical to logical transition, but you need to look at the entire I/O picture of a SQL statement, which includes looking at a statements' logical I/O as well.

- **Logical I/O** – This is a measure of how many memory reads the query took to satisfy the user's request. The goal of tuning I/O for a query should be to examine both logical and physical I/O, and use appropriate mechanisms to keep both to a minimum.

- **Repetition** – This is a measure of how often the query has been executed. A problem in this area isn't as easy to spot as the others unless you know your application well. A query that takes a fraction of a second to execute may still be causing a headache on your system if it's executed erroneously (for example, a query that executes in a runaway PL/SQL loop) over and over again

There are other criteria that you can examine, like sort activity or access plan statistics (that show items such as Cartesian joins and the like), but more often than not, these measures are reflected in the criteria listed above.

Fortunately, Oracle records all the above measures (at least 9i does), which makes tracking the SQL that's been submitted against an Oracle database a lot easier.

Pinpointing Bad SQL

When you begin to look for inefficient SQL in a database, there are two primary questions you want answered:

- What has been the worst SQL that's historically been run in my database?

- What's the worst SQL that's running right now in my database?

Historical SQL Analysis

The easiest way to perform historical SQL analysis is to use either a third-party software vendor tool, or a homegrown solution to periodically collect SQL execution statistics into a database repository, and then analyze the results. While Oracle does record SQL execution information, such data can be lost if a DBA flushes the shared pool or shuts down the database, so ad-hoc historical analysis using straight SQL scripts might produce misleading results. However, if your database is predictable in terms of SQL code being kept in the shared pool, you can certainly obtain good metrics to determine if inefficient SQL is being executed in your system.

A good 'Top SQL' script to use for Oracle9i is the *top9isql.sql* query. It will pull the top 20 SQL statements as determined (initially) by disk reads per execution, but you can change the sort order to sort on logical I/O, elapsed time, etc.:

top9isql.sql

```
select
        sql_text ,
        username ,
        disk_reads_per_exec,
        buffer_gets_per_exec,
        buffer_gets ,
        disk_reads,
        parse_calls ,
        sorts ,
        executions ,
        loads,
        rows_processed ,
```

```
        hit_ratio,
        first_load_time ,
        sharable_mem ,
        persistent_mem ,
        runtime_mem,
        cpu_time_secs,
        cpu_time_secs_per_execute,
        elapsed_time_secs,
        elapsed_time_secs_per_execute,
        address,
        hash_value
from
(select
        sql_text ,
        b.username ,
        round((a.disk_reads/
        decode(a.executions,0,1,a.executions)),2)
        disk_reads_per_exec,
        a.disk_reads ,
        a.buffer_gets ,
        round((a.buffer_gets/
        decode(a.executions,0,1,a.executions)),2)
        buffer_gets_per_exec,
        a.parse_calls ,
        a.sorts ,
        a.executions ,
        a.loads,
        a.rows_processed ,
        100 - round(100 *
        a.disk_reads/
        greatest(a.buffer_gets,1),2) hit_ratio,
        a.first_load_time ,
        sharable_mem ,
        persistent_mem ,
        runtime_mem,
        round(cpu_time / 1000000,3) cpu_time_secs,
        round((cpu_time / 1000000)/
        decode(a.executions,0,1,a.executions),3)
        cpu_time_secs_per_execute,
        round(elapsed_time / 1000000,3) elapsed_time_secs,
        round((elapsed_time /
        1000000)/decode(a.executions,0,1,a.executions),3)
        elapsed_time_secs_per_execute,
        address,
        hash_value
from
        sys.v_$sqlarea a,
        sys.all_users b
where
        a.parsing_user_id=b.user_id and
        b.username not in ('SYS','SYSTEM')
        order by 3 desc)
where
     rownum < 21;
```

Output from this query might resemble the following:

	SQL_TEXT	USERNAME	DISK_READS_PER_EXEC	BUFFER_GETS_PER_EXEC	BUFFER_GETS	DISK_READS	PARSE_CALLS	SORTS	EX
1	begin PERFCNTR_24x7_QUERIES.fetchcursor20_2(VAR1_	USR1	122.5	78886.5	157773	245	2	0	
2	SELECT 956, (INVALID_OBJECTS + UNUSABLE_INDEXES) AS TOTAL FROM (SELECT	USR1	94	45723.5	91447	188	1	0	
3	SELECT PERFCNTR_24x7_QUERIES', PERFCNTR_24x7_QUERIES.GetVersion from DUAL UNION	USR1	67	975	975	67	1	1	
4	SELECT 900, (total_space - total_free_space)/1048576 FROM (SELECT SUM(bytes) AS total_space FROM	USR1	18.5	238	476	37	1	0	
5	select 99 / 100, 1 - to_number(to_char(to_date('1997-11-0	USR1	11	86	86	11	1	0	
6	SELECT 955, COUNT(*) FROM SYS.DBA_TABLES WHER	USR1	5.5	30784	61568	11	1	0	
7	SELECT 998, COUNT(*) FROM (SELECT USERNAME FROM SYS.DBA_USERS WHERE	USR1	3.5	239.5	479	7	1	16	
8	select a.machine, b.count from (SELECT DISTINCT MACHINE FROM V$SESSION WHERE TYPE =	USR1	3	63	63	3	1	1	
9	SELECT 977, a.active active_jobs,b.due-a.active jobs_waiting,c.snp_processes - a.active idle_jobs,c.snp_processes total_jobs FROM (SELECT	USR1	2.5	70.5	141	5	1	2	
10	begin PERFCNTR_24x7_QUERIES.fetchcursor22_5(VAR1_	USR1	2.5	70.5	141	5	2	0	
11	begin PERFCNTR_24x7_QUERIES.fetchcursor16_3(VAR1_	USR1	1.67	114.5	687	10	6	0	
12	SELECT 948, ACTIVE_COUNT,ROUND(100 * (ACTIVE_COUNT / TOTAL_COUNT),2) AS ACTIVE_PCT	USR1	1.67	76.17	457	10	1	0	
13	begin PERFCNTR_24x7_QUERIES.fetchcursor1_2(VAR1_	USR1	1.33	156.17	937	8	6	0	
14	begin PERFCNTR_24x7_QUERIES.fetchcursor3_3(VAR1_	USR1	.83	107.83	647	5	6	0	

Figure 8.1 – Output from the top 20 SQL query

If you are using a version of Oracle less than 9i, you will have to modify the query above and remove the references to ELAPSED_TIME and CPU_TIME, which were new columns added to the *v$sqlarea* view in 9i.

It's important to examine the output of this query and see how it uses the criteria set forth at the beginning of this chapter to pinpoint problematic SQL.

First, start by looking at Figure 8.2 and focus on the circled columns.

	PERSISTENT_MEM	RUNTIME_MEM	CPU_TIME_SECS	CPU_TIME_SECS_PER_EXECUTE	ELAPSED_TIME_SECS	ELAPSED_TIME_SECS_PER_EXECUTE	ADDRESS	HASH_VALUE
1	540	276	1.642	.821	4.814	2.407	672621C0	3077230681
2	696	30300	.521	.26	1.204	.602	6746A26C	2985734772
3	1400	3684	.11	.11	.399	.399	674D57CC	2741343822
4	2388	22848	.06	.03	1.368	.684	6746A848	3829441909
5	700	876	.02	.02	.079	.079	674FA26C	1276527007
6	660	12748	.26	.13	.293	.147	6746A460	2911359602
7	692	100596	.05	.025	.07	.035	67469D84	3547812303
8	664	4036	.02	.02	.034	.034	674F4504	2966647892
9	852	4388	.02	.01	.054	.027	674688A0	482951707

Figure 8.2 – Output from the top 20 SQL query that shows timing statistics

The output displays both CPU and elapsed times for each query. The times are shown both cumulatively (in seconds) and per execution, indicating, for example, that the first query in the result set has accumulated almost five seconds of total execution time and runs for about two and half seconds each time it's executed.

You can change the query to sort by any of these timed statistics, depending on the criteria you need to use to bubble the worst running SQL to the top of the result set. Again, sadly, you lose these metrics when you use any database version under Oracle9i.

If you look back at Figure 8.1, you can see the columns that will help you examine the I/O characteristics of each SQL statement. You can see the number of disk reads (physical I/O) and buffer gets (logical I/O), along with numbers that display the average I/O consumption of each SQL statement.

Note that queries that have only been executed once may have misleading statistics with respect to disk reads, as the data needed for the first run of the query was likely read in from disk to memory. Therefore, the number of disk reads per execution should drop for subsequent executions and the hit ratio for the query should rise.

The executions column of the top SQL's result set will provide clues to the repetition metric for the query. When troubleshooting a slow system, you should be on the lookout for any query that shows an execution count that's significantly larger than any other query on the system. It may be that the query is in an inefficient PL/SQL loop, or other problematic programming construct. Only by bringing the query to the attention of the application developers will you know if the query is being mishandled from a programming standpoint.

Once you find the SQL statements through Oracle's diagnostic views, you will want to get the entire SQL text for the statements that appear inefficient.

You should note the HASH_VALUE values for each SQL statement, and then issue the *fullsql.sql* script to obtain the full SQL statement:

---
fullsql.sql

```
select
     sql_text
from
     sys.v_$sqltext
where
     hash_value = <enter hash value for sql statement>
order by piece;
```

Current SQL Analysis

If your phone begins to ring with complaints of a slow database, you can quickly check to see what SQL is currently executing to understand if any resource intensive SQL is dragging down your database's overall performance levels.

This is very easy to do and only involves making one change to the already discussed top9isql.sql query. You should add the following filter to the main query's *where* clause:

```
where
     a.parsing_user_id=b.user_id and
```

```
       b.username not in ('SYS','SYSTEM') and
       a.users_executing > 0
       order by 3 desc;
```

This query change will display the worst SQL that is currently running in the database, so you can quickly tell if any queries are to blame for a dip in database performance.

New Techniques for Analyzing SQL Execution

The techniques and queries showcased above are the more traditional means of pinpointing problem SQL in a database. But if you are using Oracle9i, there are some new methods you can use to get a handle on how well the SQL in your database is executing.

For example, an Oracle9i DBA may want to know how many total SQL statements are causing Cartesian joins on the system. The following *9icartcount.sql* query can answer that:

9icartcount.sql

```
select
       count(distinct hash_value) carteisan_statements,
       count(*) total_cartesian_joins
from
       sys.v_$sql_plan
where
       options = 'CARTESIAN' and
       operation like '%JOIN%';
```

Output from this query might resemble the following (note that it is possible for a single SQL statement to contain more than one Cartesian join):

```
CARTEISAN_STATEMENTS     TOTAL_CARTESIAN_JOINS
---------------------    ---------------------
                   4                         6
```

A DBA can then view the actual SQL statements containing the Cartesian joins, along with their performance metrics by using the *9icartsql.sql* query:

9icartsql.sql

```
select
      *
from
      sys.v_$sql
where
      hash_value in
(select
      hash_value
 from
      sys.v_$sql_plan
 where
      options = 'CARTESIAN'
 AND  operation LIKE '%JOIN%' )
order by hash_value;
```

Another big area of interest for DBAs concerned with tuning SQL is table scan activity. Most DBAs don't worry about small table scans, as Oracle can oftentimes access small tables more efficiently through a full scan than through index access (the small table is just cached and accessed). Large table scans, however, are another matter. Most DBAs prefer to avoid those, where possible, through smart index placement or intelligent partitioning.

Using the new 9i *v$sql_plan* view, a DBA can quickly identify any SQL statement that contains one or more large table scans, and even define 'large' in their own terms.

The following *9itabscan.sql* query shows any SQL statement that contains a large table scan (defined in this query as a table over 1MB), along with a count of how many large scans it causes for each execution, the total number of times the statement has been executed, and then the sum total of all scans it has caused on the system:

9itabscan.sql

```
select
      sql_text,
      total_large_scans,
      executions,
      executions * total_large_scans sum_large_scans
from
(select
      sql_text,
      count(*) total_large_scans,
      executions
from
    sys.v_$sql_plan a,
    sys.dba_segments b,
    sys.v_$sql c
where
      a.object_owner (+) = b.owner
and   a.object_name (+) = b.segment_name
and   b.segment_type in ('TABLE', 'TABLE PARTITION')
and   a.operation like '%TABLE%'
and   a.options = 'FULL'
and   c.hash_value = a.hash_value
and   b.bytes / 1024 > 1024
group by
      sql_text, executions)
order by
      4 desc;
```

	SQL_TEXT	TOTAL_LARGE_SCANS	EXECUTIONS	SUM_LARGE_SCANS
1	select o.owner#,o.obj#,decode(o.linkname,null, decode(u.name,null,'SYS',u.name),o.remoteowner),	1	19	19
2	SELECT 1 FROM SYS.DBA_OBJECTS WHERE ROWNUM = 1 MINUS SELECT 1 FROM SYS.DBA_EXTENTS WHERE ROWNUM = 1 MINUS	2	2	4
3	SELECT 1 FROM SYS.DBA_OBJECTS WHERE ROWNUM = 1 MINUS SELECT 1 FROM SYS.DBA_EXTENTS WHERE ROWNUM = 1 MINUS	2	1	2
4	SELECT OWNER,TABLE_NAME,NUM_ROWS,PCT_FREE,PCT_USED,TA	1	2	2
5	EXPLAIN PLAN SET STATEMENT_ID='10118429' INTO EMBARCADERO	1	1	1
6	SELECT OWNER,TABLE_NAME,NUM_ROWS,PCT_FREE,PCT_USED,TABLESPA	1	1	1
7	select count(*) from eradmin.emp	1	1	1
8	select distinct i.obj# from sys.idl_ub1$ i where i.obj#>=:1 and i.obj# not	1	1	1

Figure 8.3 – Output showing 'large' table scan activity from an Oracle9i database

This query provides important output and poses a number of interesting questions. As a DBA, should you worry more about a SQL statement that causes only one large table scan, but has been executed 1,000 times, or a SQL

New Techniques for Analyzing SQL Execution

statement that has ten large scans in it, but has only been executed a handful of times?

Each DBA will likely have an opinion on this, but regardless, you can see how such a query can assist with identifying SQL statements that have the potential to cause system slowdowns.

Oracle 9.2 has introduced another new performance view – *v$sql_plan_statistics* – that can be used to get even more statistical data regarding the execution of inefficient SQL statements. This view can tell you how many buffer gets, disk reads, etc., that each step in a SQL execution plan caused, and even goes so far as to list the cumulative and last executed counts of all held metrics.

DBAs can reference this view to get a great perspective of which step in a SQL execution plan is really responsible for most of the resource consumption. Note that to enable the collection of data for this view; you must set the Oracle configuration parameter *statistics_level* to ALL.

An example that utilizes this new 9i view is the following *9iplanstats.sql* script that shows the statistics for one problem SQL statement:

9iplanstats.sql

```
select
        operation,
        options,
        object_owner,
        object_name,
        executions,
        last_output_rows,
        last_cr_buffer_gets,
        last_cu_buffer_gets,
        last_disk_reads,
```

```
        last_disk_writes,
        last_elapsed_time
from
        sys.v_$sql_plan a,
        sys.v_$sql_plan_statistics b
where
        a.hash_value = b.hash_value and
        a.id = b.operation_id and
        a.hash_value = <enter hash value>
order by a.id;
```

	OPERATION	OPTIONS	OBJECT_OWNER	OBJECT_NAME	EXECUTIONS	LAST_OUTPUT_ROWS	LAST_CR_BUFFER_GETS	LAST_CU_BUFFER_GETS	LAST_DISK_READS	LAST
1	MERGE JOIN	CARTESIAN	[NULL]	[NULL]	1	31849	46	0	18	
2	TABLE ACCESS	FULL	ERADMIN	PATIENT	1	22	24	0	5	
3	BUFFER	SORT	[NULL]	[NULL]	1	31849	22	0	13	
4	PARTITION RANGE	ALL	[NULL]	[NULL]	1	1507	22	0	13	
5	TABLE ACCESS	FULL	ERADMIN	ADMISSION	1	1507	22	0	13	

Figure 8.4 – Example output showing statistical metrics for each step in a 9i query execution plan

SQL Tuning Roadmap

There are large volumes of SQL tuning books on the market that provide minute detail on how to build and tune SQL code. As a DBA, you can stay immersed in such manuals (and many of them are very good) for a long time, but chances are, you don't have the time.

If that's the case for you, then walk through the quick generic roadmap below, which you can use to remedy some of the problem SQL statements that you've identified using the techniques and scripts already outlined in this chapter.

Once you have one or more problem queries in hand, you can then start the tuning process, which basically consists of these three broad steps:

- Understand the query and dependent objects
- Look for SQL rewrite possibilities
- Look for object-based solutions

Understand the Query and Dependent Objects

The first thing to do is get a handle on what the query is trying to do, how the Oracle optimizer is satisfying the query's request, and what kind of objects the query is referencing.

In terms of understanding what the query is trying to accomplish and how Oracle will handle the query, the EXPLAIN plan is your first step. However, while the EXPLAIN plan has been around for as long as SQL itself, you might be surprised at how many seasoned database professionals aren't very good at reading an EXPLAIN plan output.

Now, many can do the basics like recognize table scans, spot Cartesian joins, and zero in on unnecessary sort operations, but when the EXPLAIN output "wave" starts rolling back and forth in large SQL EXPLAINs, some tend to get a little lost. Some of the better SQL analysis tools are now sporting a new EXPLAIN format (better graphics and English-based explanations) that makes it a lot easier to follow the access path trail.

For DBAs who aren't good at reading traditional EXPLAIN output, it makes getting to the root of a bad SQL statement much simpler. And it can save you or one of your developers from submitting the query from you-know-where.

If you aren't using a third-party SQL analysis product with built-in EXPLAIN functionality, then you will have to use the standard EXPLAIN plan table and methods for performing a SQL statement EXPLAIN. Users of Oracle9i, however, can get an EXPLAIN of any SQL statement that's already been executed in the database. A script like the *9iexpl.sql* can be used:

9iexpl.sql

```
select
       lpad(' ',level-1)||operation||' '||options||' '||
       object_name "Plan",
       cost,
       cardinality,
       bytes,
       io_cost,
       cpu_cost
  from
       sys.v_$sql_plan
  connect by
       prior id = parent_id
       and prior hash_value = hash_value
  start with
       id = 0 and hash_value = <enter hash value>
  order by id;
```

	Plan	COST	CARDINALITY	BYTES	IO_COST	CPU_COST
1	SELECT STATEMENT	1502	[NULL]	[NULL]	[NULL]	[NULL]
2	MERGE JOIN CARTESIAN	1502	750000	52500000	1502	[NULL]
3	TABLE ACCESS FULL PATIENT	2	500	23500	2	[NULL]
4	BUFFER SORT	1500	1500	34500	1500	[NULL]
5	PARTITION RANGE ALL	[NULL]	[NULL]	[NULL]	[NULL]	[NULL]
6	TABLE ACCESS FULL ADMISSION	3	1500	34500	3	[NULL]

Figure 8.5 – Example output for an EXPLAIN plan generated for a SQL statement already in Oracle9i's shared pool

Once you gain understanding through an EXPLAIN, you should then begin to look into the objects the EXPLAIN plan is referencing. When writing efficient SQL, it's imperative to know the demographics and shape of the objects your code will bump up against. For most databases, all the information you need is found in the data dictionary. But when querying the dictionary for object statistics, you need to make sure you're looking at accurate information.

While some databases like SQL Server 2000 have automatic updating of object statistics into the dictionary, other RDBMS engines like Oracle require you to manually (and periodically) refresh the database catalog with up-to-date object data. Fortunately, this is pretty easy to accomplish.

Oracle now offers special packages to assist with the updating of objects, in addition to the standard *analyze* command. The *dbms_utility* package contains several procedures to help database professionals update their schema objects. To update the dictionary for a single schema, you can use the *dbms_utility.analyze_schema* procedure. The *dbms_utility.analyze_database* procedure has been introduced recently for larger updates. Just be careful when executing such a procedure against a monolithic database like Oracle's applications.

Whatever method you choose to update your objects, you ought to make a practice of keeping data in the dictionary current, especially for databases that are very dynamic in nature.

Scheduling the object updates in a nightly maintenance plan would probably be a good thing to do for such a database, especially if you use the cost-based optimizer in Oracle. Fresh statistics help the optimizer make more informed choices of what path to follow when routing your queries to the requested data. Obviously, if your database thinks you only have 100 rows in a table that actually contains a million, the map used by the optimizer might not be the right one and your response times will show it.

When tuning SQL, what types of metrics should you look for in your objects to help you make intelligent coding choices? Although this list is certainly not exhaustive, for tables you can start by eyeballing these items:

- **Row counts** - No heavy explanation is needed for why you should be looking at this statistic. You will want to avoid full scans on beefy tables with large row counts. Proper index placement becomes quite important on such tables. Other reasons for reviewing row counts include physical redesign decisions. Perhaps a table has grown larger than anticipated and is now eligible for partitioning? Scanning a single partition in a table is much less work than running through the entire table.

- **Chained row counts** - Row chaining and migration can be a thorn in the side of an otherwise well-written SQL statement. Chained rows are usually the result of invalid page or block size choices (rows for a wide table just plain won't fit on a single page or block). Migration is caused when a row expands beyond the remaining size boundary of the original block it was placed into. The database is forced to move the row to another block and leaves a pointer behind to indicate its new location. While chaining and migration are different, they have one thing in common: extra I/O is needed to retrieve the row that is either chained or migrated. Knowing how many of these your table has can help you determine if object reorganization is needed. Extreme cases may require a full database rebuild with a larger blocksize. Oracle9i users, however, can create new tablespaces with larger blocksizes and move/reorganize their objects into them.

- **Space Extents** – For some databases, objects that have moved into multiple extents can be slower to access than same-size objects that are contained within a single contiguous extent of space. Later versions of Oracle, however, don't suffer from this multi-extent problem anymore, especially when objects have been placed into new locally-managed tablespaces

- **High Water Marks** - Tables that experience much insert and delete activity can be special problem children. Oracle will always scan up to a table's "high water mark", which is the last block of space it "thinks" contains data. For example, a table that used to contain a million rows, but now only has a hundred may be scanned like it still has a million! You can determine if you need to reload a table (usually done by a reorg or truncate and load) by checking the high water marks of tables to see if they still are set to abnormally high values.

- **Miscellaneous Properties** – There are several other performance boosting properties that you may want to set for tables. For instance, large tables that are being scanned may benefit from having parallelism enabled so the table can be scanned (hopefully) much quicker. Small lookup tables may benefit from being permanently cached in memory to speed access times. In Oracle, placing them into the KEEP buffer pool may do this. The CACHE parameter may also be used, although it is not as permanent a fix as the KEEP buffer pool option.

Indexes have their own unique set of items that need occasional review. Some of these include:

- **Selectivity/Unique Keys** – Indexes by their nature normally work best when selectivity is high – in other words, the numbers of unique values are many. The exception to this rule is the bitmap index, which is designed to work on columns with very low cardinality (like a Yes/No column). The selectivity of indexes should be periodically examined to see if an index that used to contain many unique values is now one that is losing its uniqueness rank.

- **Depth** – The tree depth of an index will tell you if the index has undergone a lot of splits and other destructive activity. Typically, indexes with tree depths greater than three or four are good candidates for rebuilds, an activity that hopefully will improve access speed.

- **Deleted Row Counts** – Indexes that suffer from high parent table maintenance may contain a lot of "dead air" in the form of deleted rows in the leaf pages. Again, a rebuild may be in order for indexes with high counts of deleted leaf rows.

There are of course other items you can review on the table and index statistical front, as well as at the individual column level.

Understanding the current state and shape of the objects being used in the queries you are trying to tune can unlock clues about how you may want to restructure your SQL code. For example, you may realize you haven't indexed critical foreign keys that are used over and over again in various sets of join operations. Or you might find that your million-row table is a perfect candidate for a bitmap index given the current *where* predicate.

Look for SQL Rewrite Possibilities

For complex and problematic systems, analyzing and attempting the rewrite of many SQL statements can consume a lot of a database professional's time. A book of this nature cannot possibly go into this vast subject, as there are a plethora of techniques and SQL hints that can be used to turn a query that initially runs like molasses into one that runs as fast as greased lightning.

To save time, you might want to make use of one of the third-party SQL tuning tools that can help with rewriting SQL statements. Some of these tools will even generate automatic rewrites that you can trial and review.

Some have found that using such tools can indeed cut down on the SQL tuning process if used properly, since they offer easy generation of hints and (normally) a good benchmarking facility that allows easy execution and review of performance statistics.

Even if you don't have access to third-party SQL tuning products, you can still use SQL*Plus to perform comparison benchmarks. By using the SET AUTOTRACE ON feature of SQL*Plus, you can get decent feedback from Oracle on how efficient a query is:

```
SQL> set autotrace on;
SQL> select count(*) from admission;

  COUNT(*)
```

```
 ----------
     1552

Execution Plan
 ----------------------------------------------------------
    0      SELECT STATEMENT Optimizer=CHOOSE (Cost=1 Card=1)
    1    0   SORT (AGGREGATE)
    2    1     INDEX (FAST FULL SCAN) OF 'ADMISSION_PK' (UNIQUE)
(Cost=
           1 Card=1542)


Statistics
 ----------------------------------------------------------
          0   recursive calls
          4   db block gets
          5   consistent gets
          0   physical reads
          0   redo size
        368   bytes sent via SQL*Net to client
        425   bytes received via SQL*Net from client
          2   SQL*Net roundtrips to/from client
          0   sorts (memory)
          0   sorts (disk)
          1    rows processed
```

So what are some things you should look for in terms of rewriting SQL? While this is certainly a large topic, there are a few major items that stand out above the rest:

- **The Cartesian Product** – Bob's query (see beginning of chapter), that had an estimated response time of 56 years, suffered from a terrible case of Cartesian joins. His WHERE predicate didn't contain a single correct join in the many million row tables he was trying to access. Although some optimizers will automatically try to rewrite SQL and will actually use a Cartesian product to accomplish the mission, seeing a Cartesian join in your EXPLAIN plan is usually not a good thing. If observed, check your WHERE predicate to ensure you are adhering to the N – 1 rule of thumb (for example, 10 tables in a FROM clause will require 9 proper join conditions).

- **The Table Scan** – So you thought you were using an index, did you? There are a lot of conditions that can negate the use of an index (use of NOT, failing to use the starting column of a concatenated index, use of expressions like WHERE TOTAL_SALARY = SALARY * 1.2). Or perhaps the SQL is fine, but an improper indexing scheme is being used and needs to be changed. Remember, however, that you are really looking for table scans on large tables. Small lookup tables are actually accessed many times faster when the database engine caches the whole table and scans it, rather than using an available index.

- **The Unnecessary Sort** – Can your query do without the DISTINCT clause you have in the code? Can the UNION be replaced with a UNION ALL? Knowing when and how to yank sort activity out of a SQL statement can go a long way in improving its response time.

- **The Nonselective Index Scan** - If you've followed your checklist and understand the demographics of the objects used in your query, then you should know what indexes are selective and which aren't. While cost based optimizers should ignore indexes with poor selectivity, rule based approaches may not. Be on the lookout for these types of scans because not every index scan is a good one.

When you have eliminated these noticeable coding flaws, it's now time to begin trying different code combinations in the hopes of improving your query's performance. This is where the use of hints can become a serious time saver. The SQL language now contains a plethora of hints that you can imbed in your query without really touching the actual code structure that exists. By using hints, you can in effect accomplish many iterations of rewrites in a short amount of time.

Of course, one of the dangers of using hints is not writing them accurately. Unlike typical SQL code that will cough up a syntax error if you make a mistake, an invalid hint won't afford you that luxury. *It just won't do anything.* Therefore, you need to make sure you code your hints accurately. Even the smallest of tuning techniques that use hints can produce dramatic results.

For example, one large Oracle data dictionary query that is used in this book was tuned quite well by just introducing the RULE hint to the code. It reduced the number of physical reads from 1,400 to 51, and cut the overall response time of the query in half.

So what different coding approaches should you try using hints? While there is no way to give you a complete rundown of everything that is open to you, there are a few mainstays to try:

- **The Four Standbys** – These include RULE, FIRST ROWS, ALL ROWS, and COST. Believe it or not, many times a query has been dramatically improved just by going back to the rule base optimizer. Even with all the progress made by cost-based approaches, sometimes the old way is the best way.

- **Table Order Shuffle** - You may want to influence the order in which the optimizer joins the tables used in your query. The ORDERED hint can force the database to use the right tables to drive the join operation, and hopefully reduce inefficient I/O.

- **Divide and Conquer** - When databases introduced parallel operations, they opened up a whole new avenue in potential speed gains. The PARALLEL hint can be a powerful ally in splitting large table scans into chunks that may be worked on separately in parallel, and then merged back into a single result set. One thing to ensure is that your database is set up properly with respect to having enough parallel worker bees (or "slaves") to handle the degree of parallelism you specify.

- **Index NOW** – From the EXPLAIN plan, you may discover that the optimizer is not using an available index. This may or may not be a good thing. The only way to really tell is to force an index access plan in place of a table scan with an index hint.

Look for Object-based Solutions

Object-based solutions are another option for SQL tuning analysts. This route involves things like intelligent index creation, partitioning, and more. But to do this, you have to first find the objects that will benefit from such modification, which in turn will enhance the overall runtime performance. For users of Oracle9i, the new V$ views can help with this type of analysis.

For example, if you would like to investigate better use of partitioning, you would first need to locate large tables that are the consistent targets of full table scans. The *9iltabscan.sql* query below will identify the actual objects that are the target of such scans. It displays the table owner, table name, the table type (standard, partitioned), the table size in KB, the number of SQL statements that cause a scan to be performed, the number of total scans for the table each time the statement is executed, the number of SQL executions to date, and the total number of scans that the table has experienced (total single scans * executions):

9iltabscan.sql

```
select
    table_owner,
    table_name,
    table_type,
    size_kb,
    statement_count,
    reference_count,
    executions,
    executions * reference_count total_scans
from
    (select
    a.object_owner table_owner,
    a.object_name table_name,
    b.segment_type table_type,
    b.bytes / 1024 size_kb,
    sum(c.executions ) executions,
    count( distinct a.hash_value ) statement_count,
    count( * ) reference_count
from
    sys.v_$sql_plan a,
    sys.dba_segments b,
    sys.v_$sql c
where
    a.object_owner (+) = b.owner
    and a.object_name (+) = b.segment_name
    and b.segment_type in ('TABLE', 'TABLE PARTITION')
    and a.operation like '%TABLE%'
    and a.options = 'FULL'
    and a.hash_value = c.hash_value
    and b.bytes / 1024 > 1024
group by
    a.object_owner, a.object_name, a.operation,
    b.bytes / 1024, b.segment_type
order by
    4 desc, 1, 2 );
```

	TABLE_OWNER	TABLE_NAME	TABLE_TYPE	SIZE_KB	STATEMENT_COUNT	REFERENCE_COUNT	EXECUTIONS	TOTAL_SCANS
1	ERADMIN	EMP	TABLE	19456	2	2	2	4
2	ERADMIN	PATIENT	TABLE	3496	1	1	1	1
3	ERADMIN	ADMISSION	TABLE	3136	4	7	31	217

Figure 8.6 – Identifying tables or table partitions that have been scanned in Oracle9i

The above query will help you determine what tables might benefit from better indexing or partitioning. When

---

SQL Tuning Roadmap

reviewing such output, you might begin to wonder if the tables being scanned have indexes, and if so, why don't the queries that are scanning the tables make use of them?

While only examination of the actual SQL statements can answer the second part of that question, the first part can be answered through the following *9iunused_indx.sql* query:

9iunused_indx.sql

```
select distinct
    a.object_owner table_owner,
    a.object_name table_name,
    b.segment_type table_type,
    b.bytes / 1024 size_kb,
    d.index_name
from
    sys.v_$sql_plan a,
    sys.dba_segments b,
    sys.dba_indexes d
where
    a.object_owner (+) = b.owner
    and a.object_name (+) = b.segment_name
    and b.segment_type in ('TABLE', 'TABLE PARTITION')
    and a.operation like '%TABLE%'
    and a.options = 'FULL'
    and b.bytes / 1024 > 1024
    and b.segment_name = d.table_name
    and b.owner = d.table_owner
order by
    1, 2;
```

	TABLE_OWNER	TABLE_NAME	TABLE_TYPE	SIZE_KB	INDEX_NAME
1	ERADMIN	ADMISSION	TABLE	2048	I_ADMISSION1
2	ERADMIN	ADMISSION	TABLE	2048	I_ADMISSION2
3	ERADMIN	PATIENT	TABLE	3072	I_PATIENT1
4	ERADMIN	PATIENT	TABLE	3072	I_PATIENT2
5	ERADMIN	PATIENT	TABLE	3072	I_PATIENT3

Figure 8.7 – Output showing unused indexes for tables being scanned

Such a query can create a mini "unused indexes" report that you can use to ensure that any large tables being scanned on your system have the proper indexing scheme.

Conclusion

If Bob is still out there writing SQL queries, hopefully his coding skills are much better today than they were back in 1993. By using the techniques and scripts listed in this chapter to pinpoint and correct SQL submitted by novices like him, you can hopefully prevent problem SQL from wrecking your otherwise well-performing database.

Index

A

ALL ROWS 246
ALTER INDEX ...125, 126, 164
alter session 166
alter system flush shared_pool
....158
ANALYZE.......96, 98, 127, 239
ARCH 190, 194
autoextend.....88, 89, 90, 91, 92,
   94, 99, 107
Automatic segment
   management.........83, 87, 167

B

badstorage 203
BLOB...................................85
Blocking lock ratio.................31
Bottleneck analysis ...28, 34, 35,
   42, 43, 44, 47, 48, 49, 50, 51,
   136, 199
Bubble fragmentation......83, 99,
   110
Buffer busy waits 167
Buffer cache hit ratio 13, 15, 25,
   31, 32, 60, 139, 140, 152,
   153, 175
buffer_pool_keep..........134, 147
buffer_pool_recycle 135

C

Cardinality 69, 124, 238, 242
Cartesian joins.....221, 222, 226,
   232, 233, 237, 244
Chained row counts..............240
chained/migrated rows ..85, 116,
   121, 181

CLOB...................................85
Coalesce......................103, 110
compute statistics..................96
COST...................................246
CREATE INDEX 164
cursor_sharing...............34, 159

D

Data models 9
db file scattered read..178, 215,
   216
db_block_buffers.132, 134, 143,
   176
db_cache_advice..........143, 144
db_cache_size.....134, 143, 145,
   148, 176
db_keep_cache_size.....134, 147
db_nk_cache_size........135, 148
db_recycle_cache_size........135
dbms_shared_pool...............158
DBMS_STATS....................127
dbms_utility.........................239
dbms_utility.analyze_database
....239
dbms_utility.analyze_schema
....239
DBWR 190, 194, 195
DDL command 93
Default buffer cache 134
dictionary-managed tablespace
   .... 12, 82, 83, 94, 97, 98, 104,
   111, 112, 113, 114
dispatcher timer ..36, 37, 38, 40,
   41, 177
DISTINCT..33, 44, 69, 86, 165,
   167, 245

E

enqueue 42, 178
EXPLAIN 97, 149, 224, 237, 238, 244, 247
extract-transform-load............72

F

FIRST.....................................246
fragmentation 52, 67, 68, 102, 105, 106, 108
freelists 167

G

GROUP BY 165, 190

H

hash_area_size 166
HASH_VALUE 231
High Water Mark 76, 241
Honeycomb fragmentation....83, 103

I

IN 165, 187
init.ora..................................207
initrans 167
INTERSECT 165

J

Java pool 135
java_pool_size..............133, 135
JBOD......................................78

K

Keep buffer cache 134

L

Large pool 135
large_pool_size 133, 135

latch free 156, 178
LGWR.........................190, 194
Listener process 11
lock element cleanup 36, 37, 38, 39, 41, 177
log_buffer..............133, 136, 161

M

MINUS 165

N

NOT IN....................39, 41, 165
Null event......36, 37, 38, 40, 41, 177

O

Object extent fragmentation...82
Object fragmentation ..104, 113, 115
Object-based fragmentation...86
Oracle Managed Files............84
ORDER BY 165, 190
ORDERED 247

P

PARALLEL.........................247
parallel query dequeue wait ..36, 37, 38, 40, 41, 177
parallel query idle wait - Slaves 36, 37, 38, 40, 41, 177
PCTFREE 67, 86
PCTUSED.................67, 83, 86
Performance model 9
PGA management
pga_aggregate_target......166
workarea_size_policy 166
PGA memory management..166
pga_aggregate_target...........166
pipe get...36, 37, 38, 40, 41, 177

PL/SQL lock timer....36, 37, 38, 40, 41, 177

pmon timer....36, 37, 38, 39, 41, 177

R

RAID..........................78, 84, 94

Ratio-based analysis...28, 29, 30

rdbms ipc message 36, 37, 38, 39, 41, 177

Recycle buffer cache............134

Redo log buffer 136

Row counts 240

ROWS...........................64, 246

RULE..................................246

S

SET AUTOTRACE ON 244

shared pool....33, 135, 137, 152, 153, 154, 156, 158, 159, 160, 171, 227, 238

shared_pool_size.133, 135, 137, 160

show sga..............................133

slave wait36, 37, 38, 40, 41, 177

smon timer 36, 37, 38, 39, 41, 177

sort_area_retained_size......165, 166

sort_area_size.....165, 166, 167, 176

Space Extents 241

Space fragmentation.............102

spfile...................................207

SQL Scripts

9icartcount.sql 232

9icartsql.sql.....................233

9iexpl.sql 238

9ilarge_scanusers.sql.......216

9iltabscan.sql 248

9iplanstats.sql 235

9itabscan.sql 233

9iunused_indx.sql 249

archhist.sql.......................195

badstorage.sql..................202

bgact.sql..........................194

buffratio.sql......................175

buffutl.sql 151

bufobjwaits.sql 168

cacheadvice.sql................144

cacheobjcnt.sql 150

cartsession.sql..................220

cartsql.sql........................221

chaincnt.sql......................181

chainpct.sql......................180

chaintables.sql 181

csesswaits.sql 41

curriosql.sql 219

currlwaits.sql 170

datafileae.sql.....................91

dbagranted.sql 200

dffrag.sql..........................106

dictdet.sql........................159

fileio7.sql 182

fileio8plus.sql..................182

fullsql.sql.........................231

globaccpatt.sql.................179

globiostats.sql 174

idxreorg7.sql....................122

idxreorg8.sql....................123

largescan9i.sql.................187

latchdet.sql......................169

libdet.sql..........................155

libobj.sql 156

libwait.sql........................156

lockcnt.sql 218

maxext7.sql 113

maxext8.sql 114

memhog.sql 162

memsnap.sql....137, 152, 161, 164, 165, 167, 171

objdef.sql 114
objwait.sql 42
physpctio.sql 188
poolhit.sql 140
rolldet.sql 196
scatwait.sql 215
sensprivs.sql 200
sesshitrate.sql 140
sesswaits.sql 39
sgasize.sql 132
sortdet.sql 206
sortusage.sql 205
spacesum7.sql 89
spacesum8i.sql 90
sqlhitrate.sql 142
syswaits.sql 37, 176
tabreorg7.sql 117
tabreorg8.sql 119
top9isql.sql 227, 231
topiousers.sql 191
topsess.sql 208
topsessdet.sql 211
toptables.sql 185
totpctio.sql 189
totuserspace.sql 204
tsfrag.sql 105
tsmap7.sql 108
tsmap8.sql 109
userscans.sql 214
SQL*Net break/reset to client
.... 36, 37, 38, 39, 41, 177
SQL*Net message from client
.... 36, 37, 38, 39, 41, 177
SQL*Net message to client...36,
37, 38, 40, 41, 177
SQL*Net more data to client 36,
37, 38, 40, 41
SQL*Plus 36, 133, 243
statistics_level 235
sys.dbms_space_admin 111, 112

T

table fetch continued row....179,
180
Tablespace fragmentation...107,
110, 112
timed_statistics 35

U

UNDO tablespace ..85, 168, 197
undo_management 85
UNION 165, 245
UNION ALL........................ 245
unlimited tablespace 200, 203

V

Views
v$db_cache_advice .146
v$sessstat view................. 217
v$sql_plan........................ 233
v$sql_plan_statistics........ 235
v$sqlarea................. 143, 229
v$sysstat..................... 30, 31
v_$sql_plan..... 187, 216, 221,
232, 233, 234, 236, 238,
248, 249
x$kcbrbh 146
virtual circuit status...36, 37, 38,
40, 41, 177

W

workarea_size_policy.166
Workload analysis 48, 49, 50,
51, 199, 222

The Oracle In-Focus™ Series

The *Oracle In-Focus*™ series is a unique publishing paradigm, targeted at Oracle professionals who need fast and accurate working examples of complex issues. *Oracle In-Focus*™ books are unique because they have a super-tight focus and quickly provide Oracle professionals with what they need to solve their problems.

Oracle In-Focus™ books are designed for the practicing Oracle professional. Oracle In-Focus™ books are an affordable way for all Oracle professionals to get the information they need, and get it fast.

- **Expert Authors** – All *Oracle In-Focus*™ authors are content experts and are carefully screened for technical ability and communications skills.

- **Online Code Depot** – All code scripts from *Oracle In-Focus*™ are available on the web for instant download. Those who purchase a book will get the URL and password to download their scripts.

- **Lots of working examples** – *Oracle In-Focus*™ is packed with working examples and pragmatic tips.

- **No theory** – Practicing Oracle professionals know the concepts, they need working code to get started fast.

- **Concise** – All *Oracle In-Focus*™ books are less than 200 pages and get right to-the-point of the tough technical issues.

- **Tight focus** - The *Oracle In-Focus*™ series addresses tight topics and targets specific technical areas of Oracle technology.

- **Affordable** – Reasonably priced, *Oracle In-Focus*™ books are the perfect solution to challenging technical issues.

http://www.rampant.cc/

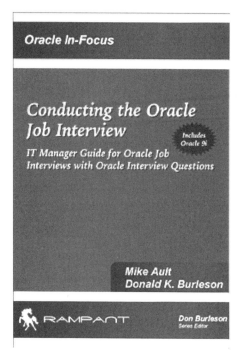

Conducting the Oracle Job Interview

IT Manager's Guide for Oracle Job Interviews with Oracle Interview Questions

Mike Ault & Don Burleson
ISBN 0-9727513-1-9
Publication Date – Feb 2003
Retail Price $16.95 / £10.95

As professional consultants, Don Burleson and Mike Ault have interviewed hundreds of Oracle job candidates. With over four decades of interviewing experience, Ault and Burleson tell you how to quickly identify acceptable Oracle job candidates by asking the right Oracle job interview questions.

Mike Ault and Don Burleson are recognized as the two best-selling Oracle Authors in the world. With combined authorship of over 25 books, Ault & Burleson are the two most respected Oracle authorities on the planet. For the first time ever, Ault & Burleson combine their talents in this exceptional handbook.

Using Oracle job interview questions that are not available to the general public, the IT manager will be able to quickly access the technical ability of any Oracle job candidate. In today's market, there are thousands of under-trained Oracle professionals, and the IT manager must be able to quickly access the true ability of the Oracle job candidate.

http://www.rampant.cc/

Oracle9i RAC

Oracle Real Application
Clusters Configuration and
Internals

Mike Ault & Madhu Tumma
ISBN 0-9727513-0-0
Publication Date - June 2003
Retail Price $59.95 / £37.95

Combining the expertise of two world-renowned RAC experts, Oracle9i RAC is the first-of-its-find reference for RAC and TAF technology. Learn from the experts how to quickly optimizer your Oracle clustered server environment for optimal performance and flexibility.

Covering all areas of RAC continuous availability and transparent application failover, this book is indispensable for any Oracle DBA who is charged with configuring and implementing a RAC clusters database.

Mike Ault is one of the world's most famous Oracle authors with 14 books in print, and Madhu Tumma is a recognized RAC clustering consultant. Together, Ault and Tumma dive deep inside RAC and show you the secrets for quickly implementing and tuning Oracle9i RAC database systems.

http://www.rampant.cc/

Creating a Self-Tuning Oracle Database

Automating Oracle9i
Dynamic SGA
Performance

Don Burleson
ISBN 0-9727513-2-7
Publication Date - March 2003
Retail Price $16.95 / £10.95

Oracle9i has become one of the world's most complex databases, and this book is for the senior Oracle DBA who needs to automate the complex mechanisms that govern the RAM memory regions of any Oracle database.

The dynamic memory features of Oracle9i make it possible to create a self-tuning database. This exciting book explores proven techniques for monitoring the behavior of the Oracle System Global Area (SGA) and shows proven techniques that can be used to anticipate upcoming problems and adjust the SGA before a performance problem occurs.

Focusing on proactive tuning and scripting, this book shows you how to collect historical data and use it to develop signatures for all memory areas. Using these metrics, you can develop scripts that will anticipate and correct upcoming SGA performance problems.

http://www.rampant.cc/

Oracle Utilities

*Using Hidden Programs, Import/Export, SQL*Loader, Oradebug, Dbverify, Tkprof and More*

Dave Moore
ISBN 0-9727513-5-1
Publication Date - June 2003
Retail Price $27.95 / £17.95

Written by one of the world's top DBAs and architect of the famous DBXray(tm) product by BMC Software, Dave Moore targets his substantial knowledge of Oracle internals at the Oracle supplied utilities. Intended for Senior Oracle professionals, these powerful utilities are hidden deep inside Oracle and Dave Moore can show you how to unleash the hidden power of these Oracle utilities.

Deep inside the operating system executables there are many utilities at the fingertips of Oracle professionals, but until now, there has been no advice on how to use these utilities. From tnsping.exe to dbv.exe to wrap.exe, Dave Moore describes each utility and has working examples in the online code depot. Your timesaving from a single script is worth the price of this great book.

.

http://www.rampant.cc/

Oracle Replication

Snapshot, Multi-master &
Materialized Views Scripts

John Garmany
ISBN 0-9727513-3-5
Publication Date - Dec 2003
Retail Price $27.95 / £17.95

This book is an indispensable reference for any Oracle DBA who must ensure the consistency of data across distributed platforms. With the advent of cheap disk and fast worldwide connectivity, many Oracle professionals recognize the benefits of distributing Oracle data. However, Oracle multi-master replication is extremely complex and time-consuming to implement. This book addresses the complexity of Oracle replication by providing working code examples and illustrations from working systems. The text covers all areas of Oracle replication, including snapshots, using dbms_job to refresh snapshots, multi-master replication and conflict resolution mechanisms.

Written by a distinguished graduate of West Point, Col. Garmany leverages his 20+ years of experience into an indispensable guide for any Oracle professional who must quickly implement Oracle snapshot and multimaster replication. A noted instructor, author and lecturer, Col. John Garmany leverages his ability to explain complex issues in Plain English into a one-of-a-kind book.

http://www.rampant.cc/